Jesus is the Head of the Church

Not 666

Symbology from the Prophecy of Revelation

Minister Glendora Shan Thomas

Jesus is the Head of the Church

Not 666

Symbology From the Prophecy of Revelation

Minister Glendora Shan Thomas

- Minister Glendora Shan Thomas -

- Minister Glendora Shan Thomas -

Dedication

This book is dedicated to our mom, Glendora Shan Thomas, and published in her memory for the advancement of the kingdom of Our Lord.

-Thomas Family

"Behold I stand at the door and knock."
(Revelations 3:20)

Table of Contents

Chapter 1: Introduction –
The Greatest Controversy of All Times

My Brothers and Sisters in Christ:

Greetings in the name of Jesus!

What is the greatest controversy of all times?

The greatest controversy of all times, throughout the entire world, is the Gospel of our LORD Jesus Christ, which is His testimony.

It is also the greatest controversy in the church of Christ.

This Gospel, or testimony, is about the man called Jesus, who is the Savior of mankind.

The Gospel relates to the world concerning:

- The birth of our LORD Jesus
- The death of our LORD Jesus
- The Resurrection of our LORD Jesus
- The ascension of our LORD Jesus

- **The second coming of our LORD Jesus**
- **The LORDSHIP of our LORD Jesus Christ**

All this controversy began with the elders of the Jews, at the time of Jesus' birth. This was in spite of all the heavenly manifestations that were revealed to so many people who lived around Bethlehem of Judea. People were discerning the signs of prophecy being fulfilled, which indicated the time of the birth of the Messiah.

On the night of Jesus' birth, shepherds were feeding their flock outside the city of Bethlehem, when they heard and saw the angels and multitude of the heavenly host, praising God for the birth of Jesus. (Luke 2:8 - 14)

Mary and Joseph presented Jesus in the temple, in obedience to the specifications of the law concerning the birth of a firstborn son, and while they were in the temple, the prophet Simeon and the prophetess Anna ministered and prophesied concerning Jesus' life. Both prophets praised God for the privilege. It was a privilege to have seen the Christ child of the nation of Israel. (Luke 2:21 - 24)

Wisemen came from the east, and asked: *"Where is He that is born king of the Jews?"* They came to give him gifts of gold, frankincense, and myrrh. (Matthew 2:1 - 11)

Yet, in spite of all this evidence, the elders of the Jews contended that Jesus could not have been the Messiah. *(They continue to sustain this argument even now!)*

They criticized Jesus intensely throughout His ministry and became violent after his death. The Pharisees, the Sadducees, the scribes, and the elders of the Jews questioned His authority as the Anointed One of God.

They said that Jesus blasphemed against God because He said that he was the Son of God, who was sent by God to preach glad tidings to the world about the kingdom of God. They were very angry with Jesus, and accused him of being a false prophet, and preaching heresy to the people.

The principal accusation at the time of his crucifixion was that he blasphemed God for the doctrine that Jesus died and called Himself the Son of God, and their Messiah. After his death, they rejected His Resurrection and His ascension. The Jewish elders and the Roman government agreed to destroy everything that pertains to Jesus Christ of Nazareth.

There were many Gentiles who did the same thing. And now there are denominations that say they believe in God but not in Jesus Christ. People continue to deny that Jesus is the Christ of God and the Son of God. These ministries who deny Him as our Savior believe that He is cursed because He died on the cross. They say that this is according to the scripture ***"Cursed is everyone that hangeth on a tree."*** **(Galatians 3:13) (Deuteronomy 21:22, 23)**

Some of these denominations do recognize Jesus as a prophet, and a teacher. There are schools of ministries whose doctrine is to reject the Gospel. They do not accept the virgin birth of Jesus. These are some of the potential reasons why the testimony of Christ is the most controversial issue throughout the world.

The Jews and the Romans persecuted the apostles and followers of Christ. They wanted to stop the move of the church and they wanted to abolish the record of Christ. Both sides acknowledge that the testimony of Christ destroys all customs and traditions that are alien to the Word of God.

Throughout the history of the Jewish ministry, they have either added or taken away substantial principles from the Law and the Commandments by changing the fundamentals of the same to replace them with principles of traditions and customs.

Jesus came to restore order to these discrepancies in the Law. He wanted to bring back the original meaning to the commandments for the sake of all the people. He wanted the people to study the scriptures, and the law of Moses, as it was given unto them without man-made ideologies, and such traditions. When the people would have achieved such understanding, then they would be able to know the principles in the Law, and they would have knowledge of the Scriptures.

Jesus came to put order to the confusion that existed about their faith, and the interpretation of the Ten

Commandments. A confusion that came about by the two theologies that ruled the synagogue at that time. This confusion was the work of the devil to defy the purpose of God for His people.

This is why the apostle John said:

"FOR this purpose, the Son of God was manifested, that He might destroy the works of the devil.

(1 John 3:8)

The Christian church stands on the testimony of Christ. Glory to God!

The controversies regarding this testimony are stronger today than at any other time in history. The enemies of Christ are stronger in their determination to defeat the purpose of Christ (the Redeemer of mankind), and the church. The Jewish hierarchy opposes the Gospel right now.

There are also Gentile hierarchies who uphold the rejection of the Gospel. The purpose in this determination is to destroy the records of Jesus' ministry. Jesus has already told us: *"The gates of hell*

shall not prevail against it." (He meant the church)
(Matthew 16:18b)

The Jewish elders and the Roman government killed Jesus. They believed that if they killed Him, they would have accomplished the deed of annihilating His teachings and scattering all of His followers.

They never accepted the fact that Jesus told them that He was the Christ, who came to fulfill His Father's will. His commission was to be the perfect sacrifice for the sin of the whole world. John the Baptist told them," *Behold the Lamb of God, which taketh away the sin of the world."* (John 1:29) But they did not care about John the Baptist either. They were more interested in finding a way to kill both Jesus and John the Baptist.

He came that the world through Him might be saved! (John 3:17)

Our salvation and redemption came through Jesus' blood shed on the cross. God, the Father, raised Jesus from the dead, according to His will, so that we might have a life everlasting through Jesus' Resurrection. Jesus ascended into heaven before the birth of the church because the Holy Spirit had to come to give life to the church. The church was born through the fire of the Holy Spirit. *(This is the fire that ignites the spirits of all the ministers and believers in the church).*

Before Jesus' death, whenever He sent out the apostles, and disciples to preach, He breathed on them to receive the power of the Holy Spirit. **(John 20:22)** Now that Jesus had risen, and He was leaving them, He reminded them to wait for the power from on high. **(Luke 24:46, 47)**

The Holy Spirit came to give birth to the ministry of the church, and they received power for the work in the Gospel. This is the anointing power to all ministers of Christ's church. That the Holy Spirit will come according to the will of God, the Father **(Acts 1:8) (Acts 2:1-2)**. And He came with fire and cloven tongues to all those who waited on Him in the Upper Room.

The Jewish priesthoods remained divided in their theologies and doctrines. Both sides were contrary regarding customs and traditions, and even in their theologies. These divisions have caused immense diversity to the meaning of the Ten Commandments. And have changed the meaning of each commandment.

The Sadducees school of theology taught that there were no spiritual things of God. ***"For the Sadducees say that there is no Resurrection, neither angel nor spirit: but the Pharisees confess both."*** (Acts 23:8)

Both priesthoods indoctrinated the people in their own principles of doctrines and traditions. So, the nation was divided into two sects of believers. Those who believed in the Pharisees' doctrine and those who believed in Sadducees' doctrine. They were also Pharisees Scribes, and Sadducees Scribes.

The Scribes were the ones who dictated the Law and were lawyers for the people. Both orders of priests were only interested in their own theology. They paid attention to the issues around them unless it affected their personal life. They did not care if the people had knowledge of the Scriptures; they wanted them to know their doctrines.

They heard John the Baptist saying: **"Prepare ye the way of the LORD. (Matthew 3:1 -4)** They acknowledged that he was the voice of one crying in the wilderness according to the prophecy of Isaiah. They acknowledged also that this term 'wilderness' represented the confusion within the religious doctrines upheld at the time, and the ignorance of the people to the Word of God. This ignorance caused the people not to have recognized their Messiah! Amen*!*

They actually ignored John the Baptist! The elders had to have recognized the signs of the time and knew the meaning of the prophecies of Simeon and Anna in the temple. But they denied this knowledge. They looked with scrutiny and disgust at the report of Jesus' birth, and disqualified Him later on, saying that He grew up in Nazareth of Galilee. They told Nicodemus the following:*Art thou also of Galilee? Search, and look for out of Galilee ariseth no prophet."* (John 7:52)

****The world is in doubt again, concerning His coming. The signs of the times are stronger each day, yet people are denying that Scriptures are being fulfilled. ****

These elders rejected Jesus' miracles. They accused Jesus and said that He did the miracles through the devil. They insisted that the virgin birth was not true, even though they studied the prophecy of Isaiah: **"Behold, a virgin shall conceive, and bear a son, and shall call his name Immanuel."** (Isaiah 7:14)

They rejected his Resurrection, knowing the Psalm that says: **"For thou wilt not leave my soul in hell; neither wilt thou suffer thine Holy One to see corruption."** (Psalm 16:10)

They proclaimed that His disciples stole his body from the tomb, because they wanted to deny His authority as the King of the Jews, and their Messiah. Both theologies disagreed constantly, and persistently, yet on issues concerning Jesus they were on one accord. Both Jewish and Roman rulers hated each other, but they joined together to crucify the LORD. They forgot their differences and worked towards a common goal, killing Jesus.

The Sadducees theology teaches that there is no Resurrection and no spiritual world. So, they denied the Resurrection, and the ascension of Jesus, most naturally! But the Pharisees who believed in the spiritual world, denied Jesus' Resurrection and ascension also!

Was this a contradiction to their theology? YES, they contradicted their own doctrine to ridicule the LORD Jesus!

The Jewish elders engaged Roman soldiers to guard Jesus' tomb. They did not want His disciples to steal His body. Jesus' words also haunted them because He had told them: ***"Destroy this temple, and in three days I will raise it up". (John 2:19)***

They gave the soldiers great sums of money to make sure that his body was not taken from the tomb. They were quick to deny that they knew how Christ would rise from the dead, according to the Scriptures. ***"Thus it behooved Christ to suffer, and to rise from the dead the third day"* (Luke 24:46) (Isaiah 53:5) (Psalm 69:9)**

But while the soldiers guarded the tomb, they noticed the stone was removed from the tomb, and were so frightened that they ran to the elders of the Jews and told them that the tomb was empty. This was what the elders had anticipated. This was their innermost fear!

This was fear that was heavy in their consciousness. ***"Destroy this temple, and in three days I will raise it up" (John 2:19)*** They purposely did not report what the soldiers told them. ***"Now when they were going, behold, some of the watches came into the city, and showed the chief priest all the things that were done. And when they were assembled with the elders, and had taken counsel, they gave large money to the soldiers, Saying, Say ye, His disciples came by night, and stole him away while we slept. And if this comes to the governor's ears, we will persuade him, and secure you. So, they took the money, and this saying is commonly reported among the Jews until this day." (Matthew 28:11 – 15)***

At the very beginning of the church many of the Sadducees, who said that they were converted to the Gospel, continued to deny the power in Jesus' Resurrection. This trend has resulted in many denominations that do not believe in the power of the Resurrection of Christ. Such denominations teach against the immortal soul of man and reject that we are spirit, soul, and body. They do not believe in angels, in demons, or the devil, and in the spirit world. They do not believe in the power of the Holy Spirit in the church for healing, and miracles today!

They believe that only those who have died in Christ, from their denominations, will hear the voice of the LORD calling them to a resurrected life forever. No other believer from any other denomination will hear that voice of the LORD.

They reject Paul's Words when he said: ***"We are confident, I say, and willing to be absent from the body, and to be present with the LORD."*** *(2 Corinthians 5:8)*

They believe that they will be the only ones who shall be called at the sound of the last trumpet, that they will be the only ones who will be given the right to live in a resurrected body with God.

They believe that the former Resurrection has already passed with Jesus. So, they look only to the second Resurrection. That only the chosen within their denomination will be the only ones who will be counted into the 144,000 going to heaven.

***Note: These 144,000 are the 12,000 from each tribe. You are safe from the nation of Israel. **(Revelation 7:4 – 8)** ***

The apostle Paul addressed these issues many times, and in the epistle to the Corinthians he said: ***"Now if Christ is not risen, then our preaching is vain, and your faith is also vain. (1 Corinthians 15:14)*** This concept was created to abolish the spiritual manifestations of the Holy Spirit in the church. This is why there are so many Christian churches who totally reject the utterance of tongues from the Holy Spirit, and other manifestations of the move of the Holy Spirit in the church today.

This is a well-established heresy that Paul warned Timothy and all other ministers against: ***"But shun profane and vain babblings: for they will increase***

***unto more ungodliness. And their word will eat as doth a canker: of whom is Hymenaeus and Philetus; Who concerning the truth have erred, saying that the Resurrection is past already; and overthrow the faith of some."* (2 Timothy 2:16-18)**

Many Jews who believe in the Pharisees' theology believe in the spiritual things of God. They believe in the Resurrection of the dead, and angels, yet they reject Jesus' is Resurrection. This rejection is the strongest weapon used to deny the power in the testimony of Christ, and the redemption of the saints of God.

This doubt is also strongly implanted within many religious bodies and is persistent within the theologies of several ministries in Christ!

This is the reason why the Body of Christ is not on one accord concerning the signs of the time, and the coming of the LORD. The body of Christ is not on one accord also concerning many issues that surround the signs, which affect our lives daily.

There are many ministers, who called themselves Servants of Christ who persistently deny the power in the Resurrection of Christ because they constantly argue about the issues that concern the proof of a resurrected body. And in so doing, they manifest doubts even about Jesus' ascension.

This type of contention weakens the faith of baby Christians, who depend on the strength of older believers to sustain them.

This contention confuses the baby Christians understanding about the faith in the Gospel. This is why the church will always contend about the Gospel because of disobedient ministers.

**A Personal Comment:

Whenever a group of subtle men meet with a determination to kill an organization, they first destroy purpose. Then they destroy the institutional testimony and objective. When these conceited actions begin to take root in the mind of the heads, these subtle men will confuse the goals that were set as the fundamental structure of the enterprise.

Then the contention plants doubt in the minds of all those who are a part of the structure. And the principle and the integrity of the organization will be contested in doubts. These destroyers continue to use their diabolic strategy by creating more confusion until the entire organization weakens from lack of strong leadership. This weakness will result in strong division and rivalry. Then when rivalry overcomes reasoning and logic, the organization is destroyed.

This is the determination of the enemies of the cross. They set out to confuse the faith in the Gospel. And Christian leaders who did not know Jesus will fall into their trap. These enemies of the cross are subtle ministers who call themselves "Men or Women of God". And when one does not know the LORD Jesus through prayer in the Holy Spirit, and the Word of God they will confuse one's faith in the Gospel.

This type of minister preys on the weak believers. They are the authors of discontentment in the church. They are the reason why there are so many Christian denominations. All denominations came into existence as a result of philosophies and discordances.

There are many scholars who have personal interpretations in the Word, which caused division in principles. Jesus said: ***"Every kingdom divided against itself is brought to desolation; and every city or house divided against itself is brought to desolation; and every city or house divided against itself shall not stand."*** **(Matthew 12:25)**

Most of these schools of thought are founded on the principle of testing the Word of God. They are like Adam. They test the Word of the LORD to see if God will perform His Word as He has spoken it. Because the objectives of these interpretations of the Gospel are to prove the determination of the Lord's Word. Adam also proved the determination of the LORD God's Word.

They are also seeking action in the Word of God. They doubt the earnestness in what he has spoken through His Word. Adam also doubted the earnestness in the LORD God 's Word when He told him: ***"Thou shalt surely die."* (Genesis 2:17)** He went on to be disobedient, and discovered that God will perform His will, according to His Word. Because God 's Word is true from the very beginning. (Psalms 119:160) Jesus said **"Heaven and earth shall pass away, but my Words shall not pass away"** (Matthew 24:35)

Let's trust in the Word of the LORD God at all times. Let's not add or take away anything from the Word of God. David said **"Thy Word have I hid in mine heart, that I might not sin against thee."** (Psalms 119:11)

The devil still plants doubts in the minds of ministers concerning the Gospel. And they in turn will use their doubts and concealed weapons, to defeat the message in the Gospel. They are not aware that they are being used to destroy the laborers in Christ.

Many ministers preach in doubt about the promises of God and cause the falling away of many believers from the Church. The believers leave the church because they are confused concerning the principles of faith. The major factors of all controversies about our faith, are based on the foundation of what we believe in the Gospel. These are:

- a virgin birth
- the death

- the Resurrection
- and the ascension of Jesus Christ

We must understand that every principle of faith stands on a true testimony. These are the true testimonies of Jesus Christ. Therefore, they are our principles of faith.

Thank you, Holy Spirit, for revelation knowledge. Without the Resurrection of the LORD Jesus Christ, there would be no hope for the Christian believer. And if we have no hope in the Resurrection, our faith in the testimony of Christ is worthless! Thank you, Jesus! **"And if Christ be not raised, your faith is vain; ye are yet in your sins."** (1 Corinthians 15:17)

The Jews deny that Jesus is the Messiah. This rejection opens the door for them to deny that Jesus is the Christ, the Anointed One of God, the Father. The Jews condemned Jesus, because Jesus said that he was sent from God, the Father, that He was the Son of God in the flesh. They said that Jesus blasphemed God and was unrighteous for saying these things. Isaiah, the prophet, said the following:

"Who hath believed our report? and to whom is the arm of the Lord revealed" *(Isaiah 53:1)*

The apostle John said:*" **He came unto his own, and his own received him not."** (John 1:11)

JESUS IS THE HEAD OF THE CHURCH: NOT 666, is very important to Christians.

It is imperative for us to understand and know who Jesus is for ourselves!
The time has come for us to recognize him, and to know that Jesus is the Son of God, who came in the flesh to redeem us unto our Father. It is not sufficient to say all these things, and not really feel this way within our spirits. For it would seem sufficient to be acquainted with Jesus by only reading the Word, and by speaking about Him, but never really knowing Him for ourselves.

We can know Jesus through prayer in the Holy Spirit, because only the Holy Spirit can take us into his presence. Prayer is the only way! The apostle Paul exalted us to pray ***"Praying always with all prayer***

and supplication in the Spirit and watching thereunto with all perseverance and supplication for all saints;" (Ephesians 6:18) The apostle Paul continue to expound prayer in this manner **"Pray without ceasing** (1 Thessalonians 5:17) and again **"Continue in prayer and watch in the same with thanksgiving."** (Colossians 4:2)

Prayer is the key to the heart of God the Father. The LORD Jesus Christ gave us this important example, throughout his ministry, because Jesus prayed all the way through until He died on the cross, uttering this last prayer: **"Father, into thy hands I commend my spirit"** (Luke 23:46)

We must pray and seek the guidance of the Holy Spirit. This is praying in the spirit, for our spirit will be on one accord with the Holy Spirit and the LORD Jesus will give us spiritual communication. We can do this only when we have been born again in the Holy Spirit; this transformation of our spirits makes us children of God.

We are then sealed by the Holy Spirit until the day of redemption, this according to the will of God, the Father. ***"But as many as received him, to them gave he power to become the sons of God, even to them that believe on his name:*** [13] ***Which were born, not of blood, nor of the will of the flesh, nor of the will of man, but of God."*** (John 1:12, 13)

God, our Father, has given us this spiritual, and heavenly communication with the Holy Spirit in Jesus! Jesus said: ***"Nevertheless I tell you the truth; It is expedient for you that I go away: for if I go not away, the Comforter will not come unto you; but if I depart, I will send him unto you.*** (John 16:17)

"Blessed be the God and Father of our Lord Jesus Christ, who hath blessed us with all spiritual blessings in heavenly places in Christ: According as he hath chosen us in him before the foundation of the world, that we should be holy and without blame before him in love." (Ephesians 1:3-4)

The Holy Spirit gives us the utterance of praying tongues as He gives us prayer if you speak before the throne of Jesus. Remember Jesus said," I and my

---

Father are one" So must our spirit be one with the Holy Spirit, should be in one accord. For Jesus His spirit was in one accord with the Father's spirit; they are one in spirit.

All ministries must be in spirit with the Holy Spirit, so that they can receive spiritual revelation in the Word, and spiritual visions from the LORD Jesus, because the Holy Spirit receives the manifestation from Jesus for the ministers in his church. And spiritual visions from the LORD. Remember, JESUS said I and my Father were in accord, for Jesus' Spirit. So must our spirit be one with the Holy Spirit, to be in my Word.

Jesus said:*" **Howbeit when He, the Spirit of truth, is come, he will guide you into all truth: for he shall not speak of himself; but whatsoever he shall hear, that shall he speak and he will shew you things to come."** **(John 16:13***)*

Throughout His ministry we will see the LORD Jesus in a light that we have never seen Him before. For we shall see Him standing mightily as LORD of lords, and KING of kings over His people. We are His people, purchased by His blood! Amen!

There are many who deny the Lord because of their religious background. And there are many people who have embraced this faith whose foundation is in the Resurrection of Christ, yet they have chosen to deny the power in Jesus's Resurrection.

Many believers are taught to believe that the Gospel is about a God who did not die on the cross. Many believe that Jesus never suffered on the cross because He was God and man in his physical existence. This is saying that Jesus never paid the price for the redemption of our souls for God, the Father.

So again, the devil is saying that our redemption came to us haphazardly, that we are redeemed from all these dead doctrines accidentally:

- adultery
- witchcraft
- sorcery
- astrology
- etc.

And that we will also enter into the kingdom of God, haphazardly and accidentally also.

We blaspheme Jesus' Death on the cross when we partake of such a belief!

It is sinful to even think in this way!

"The truth is that while we were yet sinners, Christ died for us to give us eternal life with Him in the kingdom of God." (Romans 5:8)

This fact we can never deny! *Never!*

The messengers of Satan crept into the church as messengers of light; with Satan as their lord and master, to corrupt the ministry from the very beginning of the church. This is why the apostle Paul said of these ministers the following:

" And no marvel; for Satan himself is transformed into an angel of light." (2 Corinthians 11:14)

"Therefore, it is no great thing if his ministers also be transformed as the ministers of righteousness; whose end shall be according to their works." (2 Corinthians 11:15)

These ministers deny the power of the risen Lord. They also deny the suffering of the Lord Jesus on the cross. This is why the apostles warned us so many times throughout the epistles, to study Scriptures, so we are able to go against the wiles of the devil. Remember what our LORD said to Peter. It was then that he answered *"And I say also unto thee, That thou art Peter, and upon this rock I will build my church; and the gates of hell shall not prevail against it." (*Matthew 16:18)

The church shall prevail because the devil has no power to destroy the fact that Jesus is the Christ, the Son of the living God!

The Holy Spirit revealed who Jesus was to Peter when he answered Jesus and said."*Thou art the Christ, the Son of the Living God."* (Matthew 16:16) It was then Jesus answered and said, *"Upon this rock I will build my church, and the gates of hell shall not prevail against it."* (Matthew 16:18)

This topic will manifest the labor of many false prophets and false christs, in the ministry of the church, because they are persistently confusing the principles of the Gospel. These ministers do not know the Lord Jesus Christ because they have no spiritual communication with the Holy Spirit. They have a very weak prayer life and are not before the presence of Jesus*!*

Such ministers receive very little guidance and revelation from their labor. Sometimes they lose their vision for the work and labor without a goal.

For all these reasons, they are not aware of the movement of the Holy Spirit in the church today!

- Ministers must be in the move of the Holy Spirit!
- Ministers must labor in the trend of the Holy Spirit!
- Ministers must never labor without spiritual revelation, and spiritual visions!
- Spiritual revelations only come through spiritual visions.
- Spiritual communication will come to a minister through prayer in the spirit, one in one accord with the Holy Spirit.

Ministers who labor without prayer are not acquainted with the move of the Holy Spirit! Ministers who labor without studying the Word have no revelation about the move of the Holy Spirit in the church today! They are not aware of what the Holy Spirit is saying to the church today.

Remember, the Lord Jesus told John in the prophecy of Revelation: ***"He that hath an ear, let him hear what the Spirit saith unto the churches."* (Revelation 3:22)**

So many congregations are weak in the Word because they are not operating in the move of the Holy Spirit! And they are not in the trend of the Holy Spirit.

What is the move of the Holy Spirit in the church today?

The move of the Holy Spirit in the church is how the Holy Spirit moves within the body of Christ. These manifestations are:

1. Thirst for the knowledge of the Word among believers
2. Believers yearn to be born in the Holy Spirit. They desire the utterance of tongues.

3. Believers are praying for a stronger anointing to labor for the Lord Jesus.
4. Believers are praying for the gifts of the Holy Spirit, for a stronger anointing to serve the Lord within the body.
5. There's a great revival in the church. The church is gathering more believers all over the world.
6. Miracles are in manifestation everywhere within the body.

What is the trend of the Holy Spirit?

The trend of the Holy Spirit In the spirit in the church is the way how the Holy Spirit plants seeds of faith within the hearts of the believers in the Word of God.

1. Believers are walking in the promises of God according to his Word
2. Believers are claiming the Word of God and living righteously and in obedience to the Commandments of Christ.
3. The revival of the old paths. Living for the manifestation of the Word of God in one's life.

4. Believers know who they are in Christ and live in the reality of the Word in their life.
5. Believers study the Word for spiritual knowledge of Jesus Christ.
6. Believers are committed to the Word.
7. Believers are praying with covenant prayer partners in the LORD Jesus.
8. Believers are seeking the presence of Jesus in prayer through the Holy Spirit.
9. Believers desire the Rhema Word.

Ministers must know what the Holy Spirit is saying to the churches at all times! They should know how he is planting the seed of the Word in the hearts of the people of God.

We must not have weak ministries in Christ!

The people of God must believe in the Word and have blind faith in God. Believers must be on one accord in Christ. We cannot cling entirely on excerpts from great scholars. We must cling more to the revelations of the Holy Spirit.

Let us not entertain the antichrist leopard ministry in our churches, by being confused about the promises of Christ. The Word of God is simple once we are blessed with spiritual understanding in the revelation of the mysteries of God's Word.

** Note:

False teachers understand that misconceptions are keys to destruction. Jesus has spoken the Word against the destruction of His church. Jesus destroyed the works of the devil, when he said: "And the gates of hell shall not prevail against it" The Words of the Lord stand forever! Amen.

Jesus was manifested for one purpose to destroy the works of the devil ***"For this purpose the Son of God was manifested, that he might destroy the works of the devil. (1 John 3:8)***

This is why it is so expedient for a minister to have a faithful steady life in the Holy Spirit. So, they are able to recognize the leopard ministry's suggestions. The leopard ministry's theme is:

Destroy the church! *But not so, said the Lord Jesus Christ! Amen!*

The apostle Paul said to Timothy: ***"Study to shew thyself approved unto God, a workman that needeth not to be ashamed, rightly dividing the Word of truth."*** **(2 Timothy 2:15)** We divide the Word of truth without the anointing of the Holy Spirit! Anointing comes only through studying and meditation in the Word.

With prayer, prayer, prayer!

We must never stray from the truth, but always contend for the faith, which was delivered unto us by the holy apostles, through prayer. So that the Holy Spirit can guide us in our labor, every step of the way!

The apostle Jude has emphatically told us to do this: ***It was needful for me to write unto you and exhort you that ye should earnestly contend for the faith which was once delivered unto the saints."*** **(Jude: verse 3)**

Your Sister in Christ,

Minister Glendora Shan Thomas

February 16, 1998, p.m.

"Behold I stand at the door and knock."

(Revelations 3:20)

Chapter 2:

Jesus Christ,

the Anointed One of the Father

"And this Jesus, whom I preach unto you, is Christ. "
(Acts 17:3)

THE BIRTH OF THE LORD JESUS:

Is the identification for the LORD Jesus Christ. This is the birth of the man called Jesus, the Christ of God.

1 – This is the Image of Christ.

For He is the Christ of God, the Father

"And in the sixth month the angel Gabriel was sent from God unto a city of Galilee, named Nazareth, to a virgin espoused to a man whose name was Joseph, of the house of David; and the virgin's name was Mary." **(Luke 1:27)**

"And behold, thou shalt conceive in the womb, and bring forth a man son, and shall call his name JESUS. "He shall be great, and shall be called the Son of the Highest: and the Lord God shall give unto Him the throne of His father David:" (Luke 1:32)

This is the LORD Jesus, a baby that was born of a virgin, through the power of the Holy Ghost. He was the Son of Man, because He was born of a woman, with flesh and blood, and all the qualities of a man. The prophet Isaiah wrote the following about Jesus:

"[2] For he shall grow up before him as a tender plant, and as a root out of a dry ground: he hath no form nor comeliness; and when we shall see him, there is no beauty that we should desire Him. He is despised and rejected of men; a man of sorrows and acquainted with grief: and we hid as it were our faces from him; he was despised, and we esteemed him not. Surely, He hath borne our griefs, and carried our sorrows: yet we did esteem him stricken, smitten of God, and afflicted. But he was wounded for our transgressions, he was bruised for our iniquities: the

***chastisement of our peace was upon him; and with his stripes we are healed."* (Isaiah 53:2-5)**

Jesus is the Anointed One of the Father, the Christ of God. The Spirit of the LORD God was upon Him, the Holy Spirit! The man Jesus came by birth through the Holy Spirit, for he was born of the Holy Spirit, who is the LORD, the LORD God, the Holy Spirit. The third person of the Trinity. The Holy Spirit planted the holy seed into Mary's womb. ***"The Holy Ghost shall come upon thee, and the power of the Highest shall overshadow thee: therefore, also that holy thing which shall be born of thee shall be called the Son of God."* (Luke 1:35)**

Therefore the LORD Jesus was anointed from the womb to do the will of the Father, by the Holy Ghost. But not until he was baptized by John the Baptist, was He able to use this anointing that was given to Him. For coming out of the water, the Holy Ghost came up over Him in the shadow of a dove, to confirm the calling on His life. Then He went forward with the task that was before Him on this earth.

This was the beginning of the great ministry of the

Resurrection and reconciliation in the salvation of all mankind. ***"And Jesus, when He was baptized, went up straightway out of the water: and, lo, the heavens were opened unto Him, and He saw the Spirit of God descending like a dove, and lighting upon Him: And lo a voice from heaven, saying, This is my beloved Son, in whom I am well pleased. "*** **(Matthew 3:16, 17)**

Jesus had to be tested, and tried by the Holy Ghost. He had to face the devil also. Jesus had to face the wilderness of life, and know what is:

- the lust of the flesh
- the lust of the eye
- and the pride of life

The man Jesus had to humble Himself and become totally obedient to the direction of the Holy Spirit.

Remember when the children of Israel journeyed in the wilderness, how the LORD God brought them through this ordeal to humble them, and to prove them, so that they would acknowledge Him. They needed to know how well they were grounded in the commandments of the LORD God.

And so, at the end of their journey they came into the realization of which way they would go in the LORD God. The LORD God also told them about the consequences of their disobedience. They had to make a choice.

Deuteronomy tells us the following: ***"And He humbled thee, and suffered thee to hunger, and fed thee with manna, which thou knewest not, neither did thy Father's know; that He might make thee know that man doth not live by bread only, but by every Word that proceedeth out of the mouth of the LORD doth man live."*** **(Deuteronomy 8:3)**

Likewise, every ministry which is ordained by the Holy Ghost must go through a wilderness. This is the time of trial. Every minister must be tried, so that one can acknowledge one's strength to uphold the commandments of the LORD. This strength must come from within if one is grounded in the Word. A minister must know how to face the challenges of the ministry.

One must realize that the challenges in the labor of the LORD cannot be faced by one's strength but in the strength of the Word of God. David said: ***"God is our refuge and strength, a very present help in trouble."*** **(Psalm 46:1)** Remember Jesus' strength came from PRAYER! Ministers must do the same: Pray always in the Holy Spirit.

Paul said: ***"Put on the whole armor of God, that ye may be able to stand against the wiles of the devil. For we wrestle not against flesh and blood, but against principalities, against powers, against the rulers of the darkness of this world, against spiritual wickedness in high places."*** **(Ephesians 6:11,12)**

The Christ-like spirit in Christ, had to be on one accord with the Holy Spirit, in order to create the greatest miracle of deliverance since the creation of man. The miracle was the birth of the new creation of the children of God, being born again through the power of the Holy Spirit. We were transformed at our confession of faith in Christ, Jesus. ***"That if thou shalt confess with thy mouth the Lord Jesus, and shalt believe in thine heart that God hath raised him from the dead, thou shalt be saved. (Romans 10:9)***

This labor of salvation for man had to be done by one in whom there was no sin. Our LORD Jesus was born of an incorruptible seed. By the power of the Holy Spirit. He was manifested in the earth to do the will of the Father, and was commissioned to bring about the Father's will and purpose for man in the earth. And that is: ***"but that the world through him might be saved." (John 3:17b)***

The controversy of the virgin birth of our LORD Jesus is one of the greatest means of blasphemy used by the leopard ministry against the authority of Christ in the church. This ministry laughs about Jesus' birth. They justify themselves by saying that no one is born contrary to the law of natural reproduction. They say that Christians are foolish to believe that JESUS was born of a virgin.

However, there are Christians who say the same thing about the virgin birth. This is the plan of the wicked, to challenge the truth of the Gospel. It is so sad to think that some of them call themselves followers of Christ. This is only one of the many contentions of the spotted ministries existing in the church. This is the leopard spoken of in Revelations: ***"And the beast which I saw was like unto a leopard."* (Revelations 13:2) *"And he opened his mouth speaking great things and blasphemies."* (Revelation 13:6)**

The apostle Jude said of these ministries the following: ***"These are spots in your feasts of charity, when they feast with you, feeding themselves without fear. (Jude, verse 12)***

The apostle Peter also called him spots. ***"Spots they are and blemishes, sporting themselves with their own, deceiving while they feast with you."* (2 Peter 2:13)** This is distortion. It is the highest blasphemy in the ministry of Christ. This is why the LORD Jesus will come for a church without spot or blemish: ***"That he might present to himself a glorious church, not having spot, or wrinkle, or any such thing; but that it should be holy and without blemish."* (Ephesians 5:27)**

This is total denial of the man, who is the Christ, the Anointed One of the Father.

At the very beginning of Christ's ministry, He stood up in the temple and identified Himself. He read from the prophecy of Isaiah ***"The Spirit of the Lord God is upon me; because He hath anointed me to preach the Gospel to the poor, he hath sent me to bind up the brokenhearted, to preach deliverance to the captives, and recovering of sight to the blind, to set at liberty them that are bruised, To preach the acceptable year of the LORD."*** (Luke: 4:18)

They expected the Messiah. They knew that He shall be the Anointed One of God; the Christ who will come to them with healing in His wings. So many signs and wonders had happened in the cities around Nazareth for a period of years. Herod, the king, was so troubled in his spirit, after he spoke to the wiseman that he sent and killed the boy children two years old and under, hoping to kill the king of the Jews! Because this is what the wise men called the child: ***"There came wise men from the east to Jerusalem, saying, Where is he that is born King of the Jews?"*** (Matthew 2:1b,2a)

Yet many people pretended not to have recognized the King of the Jews when He began His ministry. They had seen the signs; they had witnessed the shepherds' vision of the angels singing at Jesus' birth. **(Luke 2:13 -18)**

They had heard the prophecy of Simeon, (Luke 2:26 - 32) and Anna in the temple, (Luke 2:36 -38) and most of all they knew the scriptures of Isaiah that foretold His life among them. They read the scriptures from Isaiah every Sabbath. Yet they hardened their hearts and rejected him; they couldn't care less.

We do the same thing today! We are witnessing signs of His coming, yet we deny them! We are absolved in our own interpretations of scriptures just like they were, but not absolved in the revelations of the Holy Spirit, and the signs of the time. This is why there are so many churches who are paying attention to the move of the Holy Spirit. Glory to God! Anna spoke of Him to all those who looked for the redemption in Jerusalem.

"And there was one Anna, a prophetess, the daughter of Phanuel, of the tribe of Asher: she was of a great age, and had lived with an husband seven years from her virginity; And she was a widow of about fourscore and four years, which departed not

from the temple, but served God with fasting and prayers night and day. And she is coming in that instant gave thanks likewise unto the Lord, and spake of him to all them that looked for redemption in Jerusalem." (Luke 2:36 – 38)

The Pharisees and the Sadducees, both priesthood and the religious people preached about Moses, yet they did not foresee the parallelism in Herod's plight to kill all of the boys who were two years old and younger. Herod was doing the same thing Pharaoh did at the time of Moses' birth.

The devil used Pharaoh to defeat Joseph's prophecy to the nation of Israel, because he recognized that the Deliverer had come to the nation of Israel, just as Joseph had prophesied. Now the devil was using Herod to defeat the savior of all mankind. Joseph has said: *"And Joseph took an oath of the children of Israel, saying, God will surely visit you, and ye shall carry up my bones from hence"* (Genesis 50:25)

Both Pharaoh and Herod were overcome by the fear of losing their authority over the Jewish nation. They knew that the Jews are the called nation of God. They knew that the Word of God was planted within this nation, for the Jews were commissioned by the Lord God to teach the Word of God to the whole world. This nation is the vineyard of God ***"For the vineyard of the Lᴏʀᴅ of hosts is the house of Israel, and the men of Judah his pleasant plant:"*** **(Isaiah 5:7a)**

It is written in Revelation: ***"Thrust in thy sickle and reap: for the time is come for thee to reap; for the harvest of the earth is ripe."*** **(Revelation 14:15b)** This seed of the Word of God must yield fruit for the harvesting of the saints. The chosen priesthood of the Lord God of Israel was constituted upon the principles and structure of the heavenly priesthood. This priesthood was called and ordained in the wilderness by Moses, according to the will of the Lord God. It was instituted for the nation of Israel and the world. ***"Now therefore, if ye will obey my voice indeed, and keep my covenant, then ye shall be a peculiar treasure unto me above all people: for all the earth is mine."*** **(Exodus 19:5)**

Pharaoh and Herod recognized that in spite of being the chosen vessel of the Lord God, the people are stubborn in their obedience to the Word of God, and they do not accept the Lord Jesus Christ as their Messiah.

The devil knows if they are pregnant with the Word, they will be in travail, and not give birth to the fruits of their labor, until they have come into the knowledge of the Gospel of Christ. The devil knows that God will perform His will in the wicked nations, through the nation of the Jews, because God's Word must be fulfilled. God's Word will not return void unto Him, it shall accomplish His will. **(Isaiah 55:11)** The Word of God is established through this nation, as it was spoken by the LORD God. And written through the inspirations of the holy prophets in the anointing of the Holy Spirit. Remember always: ***"salvation is of the Jews."*** Words of the LORD Jesus Christ! **(John 4:22)**

The wise men told Herod they came to see: ***"He that is born king of the Jews."*** **(Matthew 2:1)** This was an awakening to Herod's innermost fear! Let's not fool ourselves. Herod knew about the birth of the KING of the Jews. Because he believed in astrology and the oracles. He also believed in seers, who had warned him about this king of the Jews!

Moses' words were the awakening to Pharaoh's innermost fear.. Pharaoh Pharaoh also believed in the oracles and the seers because he looked to astrology for the future predictions. Pharaoh knew the Deliverer was born to the Hebrews. Pharaoh also knew that Joseph's prophecy was about to come to pass.

Let's not forget that all pharaohs were taught by tradition that Joseph was a great prophet of this nation, so they lived in expectation of the prophecy being fulfilled. And feared the day when it would happen! This is why he killed the boys two years old and younger! **(Exodus 1:1-22) (Exodus 2:1-10)**

Remember Job also had an innermost fear. He said: ***"For the thing which I greatly feared is come upon me, and that which I was afraid of is come unto me."*** **(Job 3:25)** We have all had innermost feelings about many things in our life. But now that we have been born again, we have the Holy Spirit who gives us all direction! Our fears are all in the hands of Jesus. Just smile in the joy of the LORD! Amen! For the joy of the Lord is our strength! ***"For the joy of the Lord is your*** *strength."* **(Nehemiah 8:10)**

> Oh, thank you Jesus, who gave us the victory
> And thank you Holy Spirit, for staying with us always
> until Jesus comes!
> Oh Hallelujah LORD Jesus!
> Praise you LORD, Holy Spirit!
> Glory to the Father, in Jesus mighty name!!!
> Amen! And praise God……

The people did not care to listen to John the Baptist. They did not want to hear what he had to say to them. He was the voice of one crying in the wilderness, **"Prepare ye the way of the Lord, make his paths straight."** (Luke 3:4)

"The voice of him that crieth in the wilderness, Prepare ye the way of the Lord, make straight in the desert a highway for our God "(Isaiah 40:3)

John the Baptist preached about the Lord Jesus, for he was the forerunner of Christ. He was the angel who did it before the LORD to prepare his way before the people. John the Baptist prepared the people with the baptism of repentance, to receive the message of

---

Christ. He preached about the Lord by telling the people about the Lord's miraculous works. John the Baptist came in the spirit and power of Elijah: ***"And he shall go before him in the spirit and power of Elijah, to turn the hearts of the fathers to the children, and the disobedient to the wisdom of the just; to make ready a people prepared for the Lord."*** (Luke 1:17)

"Behold, I will send you Elijah the prophet before the coming of the great and dreadful day of the LORD; And he shall turn the heart of the fathers to the children, and the heart of the children to their fathers, lest I come and smite the earth with a curse." (Malachi 4:5,6)

The Jews knew the scripture which prophesied the coming of the prophet Elijah before the coming of the Messiah. They also knew that the angel who gave these were the prophecy to John's father, Zachariah, at the time of his birth ***"And he shall go before him in the spirit and power of Elias"*** (Luke 1:17)

They saw John the Baptist as Elijah, because of the anointing power and message in his ministry. He told them that Jesus would baptize them with the fire of the Holy Ghost. Therefore, ignorance is not the cause of their negligence to recognize the Lord Jesus Christ.

Ignorance is never the cause for ministers to not know the Lord 's plan. For the Lord reveals his plan to His ministers first, to alert His people.

- **"Surely the Lord God will do nothing, but he revealeth his secret unto his servants the prophets."(Amos 3:7)**

They also had the evidence of the Lord's baptism as the Holy Spirit descended upon him in the form of a dove. Doves represent peace, freedom, and love. And those who were witnesses heard the voice of the Father when he said, **"This is my beloved Son in whom I am well pleased."** (Matthew 3:17) Jesus always had an open ministry before all the people. *(Jerusalem has always been a cosmopolitan city.)*

He traveled throughout the entire region from city to city preaching the Gospel. And this should have been the peoples' wakeup call. Moreover, Jesus did many miracles and showed them signs which should have been clues for them to have recognized Him!

But it was not so, because religion and doctrine ruled the hearts of the elders. Let's remember when Jesus called Lazarus from the dead how people believed in him. Have we ever stopped and wondered why all of a sudden, they were looking at him in a different light? Could it have been because they saw the glory of the Father in Jesus.... Just imagine the brightness of the glory of God, the sun, manifesting itself on the countenance of Christ of God, before all those people!

Awesome…. Awesome…. Awesome

"Jesus prayed this prayer to the father "*Father I thank thee that thou hast heard me. And I know that thou hearest me always: but because of the people which stand by I said it, that they may believe that thou hast sent me.*" (John 11:41, 42)

What did Jesus say until Martha: **"*Said I not unto thee that if thou wouldest believe thou shalt see the glory of God. Yes, the message is:*" Believe and be established."** The people then believed that salvation had come. Because it was in that instant, the Words of John the Baptist came alive in their hearts: **"*Behold the Lamb of God, that taketh away the sin of the world.*" (John 1:29)** They agreed with the Romans to kill Jesus. They did not want Jesus to correct the traditions and customs which they held in contrast to the law and the commandments. Jesus was a liberator and spread new ideas to the Roman people.

These principles were in regard to the interpretation of the law, and the commandments. These priests disagreed about everything and caused confusion among the people.

Many of these conflicts exist within the contentions of the various denominations in the body of Christ. These conflicts were introduced to the body of Christ by these two groups of priests after they were converted into the ministry of Christ. **(Acts 15:1-41)** This confusion is one of the elements that has always strengthened the anti-Christ movement in the church.

The council of the apostles about the Gentiles' obligation in the church recorded in the book of Acts is still ignored by denominations who have had their own origin from these two sects. **(Acts 15:1 -29)**

Examples of issues discussed by the apostles at the council are:

- That Christians should not worship on the Sabbath day. They agreed that Christians should worship on the first day of the week. This is the day of Jesus' Resurrection!

- That Gentiles should not eat as usual and not according to the Jewish law. The Gentiles should abstain and not eat any meat that was sacrificed unto idols!

- Etc.,

Christians are not under the law of Moses. This is why the apostle James said ***"For whosoever shall keep the whole law, and yet offend in one point, he is guilty of all."*** These are factors that have altered many profound teachings in the Gospel.

The apostle Jude said of these anti-Christ ministers the following: ***"But these speak evil of those things which they know not: but what they know naturally, as brute beasts, in those things they corrupt themselves."***(Jude, verse **10)**

"These are spots in your feasts of charity, when they feast with you, feeding themselves without fear: clouds they are without water, carried about of winds; trees whose fruit withereth, without fruit, twice dead, plucked up by the roots; (Jude, verse 12)

The Sadducees were the ones who gave the first argument on the Resurrection of the LORD Jesus. They denied His Resurrection totally. This is the second controversy in the hierarchy of the Jewish church concerning our LORD Jesus. This is why the apostle Paul never ceased to write about the Resurrection of the LORD Jesus Christ, when he spoke about the issue of Jewish unbelief. **(Romans 10:1-21)**

He warned the church of Christ constantly not to be established in unbelief while taking heed to the Jewish unbelief. This blasphemy of the LORD's power in his Resurrection gives the devil the instrument to destroy our faith in the key principle on which Christ's Church stands. Our Resurrection!........

Our faith is founded on the Resurrection of Christ, of the Christ of God!

Our faith is upon the image of Christ'

THE IMAGE OF THE CHRIST OF GOD

This faith is given to us by God, Father, for us to defeat the wiles of the devil! Glory to the Father!

This blasphemy is used to defy Jesus' words to the disciples: ***"All power is given unto me in heaven and in earth."*** **(Matthew 28:18b)** The followers of such denominations do not believe that we are spirit soul and body.

They believe: "what you see is what you get" They believe also: "Seeing is believing!"

They deny the foundation of the Gospel which is the glad tidings of our soul's salvation Jesus said: ***"In your patience possess ye your souls."*** **(Luke 21:19)**

Jesus also said: ***"And fear not them which kill the body, but are not able to kill the soul: but rather fear***

him which is able to destroy both soul and body in hell." (Matthew 10:28*)*

Therefore, this heresy denies the reason for the manifestation of Christ on the earth!

The apostle Paul said: **"And if Christ be not risen, then is our preaching vain, and your faith is also vain." (1 Corinthians 15:14)** The Resurrection of the Lord Jesus is the turning point of all other doctrine, and the traditions of dead other doctrines of the dead were established on:

- The REincarnation

- The wandering spirit of the dead throughout the universe

- Purgatory

The religion of the dead is divided into several sectors, all cater to idols, demonic worship and witchcraft

The LORD God told the children of Israel not to become involved in these religions when they reach the promised land. But the nation was disobedient to His Word and became involved in idol worship. These religions are founded on traditions and customs.

The LORD God warned the Israelites to remain faithful to His commandments, and worship Him only and not to worship idols. **(Exodus 20:1 – 26)**

He never gave them an image of Himself when he spoke to them from the mountain. They heard His voice and saw fire on Mount Sinai. As He spoke to them they saw the light of His glory. **(Exodus 24:1 – 18)**

The prophet Moses asked the LORD God to let him see His glory, and the Lord gave Moses a glimpse. as the LORD passed by Moses and allowed him to see Him backward **(Exodus 34: 1- 35).** The LORD God of Israel instructed the children of Israel to live only by His commandments. He also told Moses that they would disobey His instructions.

He told Moses to tell them the following *"Set your hearts unto all the Words which I testify among you this day, which ye shall command your children to observe and to do, all the Words of this law. For it is not a vain thing for you: because it is life, and through this thing ye shall prolong your days in the land, whither ye go over Jordan to possess it."* **(Deuteronomy 32:46b-47)**

The priests became dogmatic and traditional. They even added customs to the interpretation of the law, and the words of the Ten Commandments. When Jesus came He was troubled by these traditions, and doctrines in the Law and in the interpretation of the Commandments. He constantly spoke out against them in the temple. Jesus' actions were rejected by the hierarchy of the Synagogue. The people were not taught the prophetic Word. They did not have a proper understanding of the scriptures. The elders were angry at Jesus' accusations, and never accepted His rebuke. In an attempt to ridicule Jesus all the time these religious leaders refused to hear his message from the Father. Jesus was accused of blasphemy, because he said ***"They are not of the world, even as I am not of the world."*** **(John 7:16)** These controversies to which I refer are greater than we can understand without the spiritual guidance of the Holy Spirit. These controversies are within both Jewish and the Gentile communities of faith.

There are ministers of Christ who deny the anointing of the Holy Spirit in the church today. This is the very foundation of the church because the church was not birthed without the anointing of the Holy Spirit. **(Acts 2:1 -4)**

Where there is no anointing, there is no power to preach the Gospel.

If Jesus wanted a dead church, the Holy Spirit would not have come to the church from the Father!

The Jews disobeyed the Word of the LORD God of Israel. They worshiped idols in the promised land. The LORD God had told Moses that they would do this, but he also told him about his consequences: ***"And the LORD said unto Moses, Behold, thou shalt sleep with thy fathers; and this people will rise up, and go a whoring after the gods of the strangers of the land, whither they go to be among them, and will forsake me, and break my covenant which I have made with them." (Deuteronomy 31:16)***
So all the traditions, superstitions, and diversity of philosophical doctrine came to them from other religions.

*****Please note**
Every established priesthood is responsible for the edification of God's people: *"And he gave some,*

apostles; and some, prophets; and some, evangelists; and some, pastors and teachers; For the perfecting of the saints, for the work of the ministry, for the edifying of the body of Christ: Til we all come in the unity of the faith, and of the knowledge of the Son of God, unto a perfect man, unto the measure of the stature of the fullness of Christ." **(Ephesians 4:11 – 13)**

The Levitical priesthood was commissioned to do the same thing for God's people all over the world. They were accused of witchcraft.

***** Please note the following statements**
This quote was taken from **Temple written by Alfred Edersheim**. *The Officiating Priesthood, chapter 4: page 94*

"But in the second temple they got the high priestess for money: and those who say they destroyed each other by witchcraft."

The book of Ezekiel speaks strongly about priesthood,idolatry, and witchcraft. **(Ezekiel 8:7-11)**
- o   Witchcraft is the religion of idol worshipers.

- o Witchcraft is a testimony of many doctrines around the world.
- o Witchcraft has picked up momentum among the nations of the world.
- o Many Christian denominations have adopted witchcraft practices!
- o

Sadly, witchcraft has become a dominant factor within many Christian ministries. The leopard ministry is influencing the church and it consists primarily of ministers that do not know the Holy Spirit!

The apostle Jude said:*" **These be they who separate themselves, sensual, having not the Spirit."** (Jude, verse 19)*

Witchcraft practitioners no longer operate secretly. They are open to all who seek them.

No one hides to consult a psychic anymore. The psychic centers are part of the community services.

This subject should be strongly rejected in the church, so as to alert congregations against this blasphemy in the presence of Christ. But the church stands guilty of these practices. Therefore, the church cannot condemn witchcraft.

This is one of the controversies in the church!

Witchcraft is used to destroy the image of our dear Lord and Savior Jesus Christ. It is the devil's testimony and image, as opposed to the Gospel, the testimony and image of Christ.

***Remember always that the church of Christ is not a religion:

1 – IT IS FAITH BY THE GRACE OF GOD TO JESUS CHRIST OUR LORD!

2 – THIS FAITH IS ACCORDING TO THE WILL OF GOD, THE FATHER!

3 –IT IS THE MANIFESTATION OF THE WILL OF GOD IN THE EARTH, FOR THE REDEMPTION OF ALL MANKIND IN THE EARTH!......

4 – For this reason we are the children of God, through Jesus Christ.

Remember, the prophecy of revelation said: ***"And they overcame him by the blood of the Lamb, and by the Word of their testimony; and they loved not their lives unto death." (Revelation 12:11)***

Our testimony is the Gospel of Christ!

Thank you, Holy Spirit for revelation knowledge!

Why does witchcraft in all these phrases destroy the image of the Lord Jesus?

- Because it is the direct dissension of the Gospel.
- It is the devil's greatest weapon against the children of God.
- The devil has made it into many religions around the world.
- These religions have a diversity of believers.

Witchcraft is so well organized that its ministry remains alive and well in the ministry of Christ.

Ministers of Christ who follow after witchcraft are bold about their actions. They are found within the hierarchy of Christ's priesthood. They argue about the scriptures constantly to justify their actions. They pretend that they know a lot more about the Scriptures than the Holy Spirit who wrote the Scriptures.

The apostle Paul speaks a lot about the scoffers and the ministers of Satan, who have infiltrated the Body of Christ. He said that they crept into the church unawares from the very beginning of its movement. They have set up themselves as teachers, evangelists, pastors, prophets, and apostles.

They are the ministry of the antichrist.

The apostle Paul spoke to the church at Thessalonica about the manifestation of the antichrist in the church:

"Let no man deceive you by any means: for that day shall not come, except there come a falling away first, and that man of sin be revealed, the son of perdition; Who opposeth and exalteth himself above all that is called God, or that is worshiped; so that he as God sitteth in the temple of God, shewing himself that he is God." **(2 Thessalonians 2:3,4)**

"And then shall that wicked be revealed, whom the Lord shall consume with the spirit of His mouth and

shall destroy with the brightness of his coming Even Him, whose coming is after the working of Satan with all power and signs and lying wonders." (2 Thessalonians 2:8-9)

"Behold I stand at the door and knock"
(Revelation 3:20)

Chapter 3:

Let Us Consider These Heresies of the Gospel

THE GOSPEL IS THE TESTIMONY OF CHRIST:

The Mark of Christ

THE DEATH OF OUR LORD JESUS CHRIST
Him, being delivered by the determinate counsel and foreknowledge of God, ye have taken, and by wicked hands have crucified and slain." (Acts 2:23)

I have already spoken about the Jews saying that the disciples stole the body of Christ to justify their denial that He is the Christ of God, and that they do not want Jesus to be their Messiah. (Matthew 28:11 – 15)

Nevertheless, our LORD Jesus Christ was received by those who looked for redemption in Jerusalem, as the prophetess Anna spoke to them (Luke 2:36 – 38). They are the ones who followed Christ and ministered unto Him throughout His ministry. They are among the first believers in the church!

Many of them were among the 120 ministers, who received final instructions from the Lord Jesus in the Upper Room. They were with the apostles, and the disciples waiting to meet the Holy Spirit on the day of Pentecost.

Jesus taught them how to administer the church under the admonition of the Holy Spirit.

I have also spoken about the dispute that the apostle Paul had with the Jews concerning the hope of the believer's salvation, which is the Resurrection of our LORD Jesus Christ.

The Pharisees, the Sadducees, and the Scribe rejected Jesus, and did not receive HIM! They will not accept Him as the Anointed One of the Father. The Christ of God!

"Paul was pressed in the Spirit and testified to the Jews that Jesus was the Christ. And when they opposed themselves and blasphemed, he shook his raiment and said unto them, our blood be upon your own heads; I am clean, from henceforth

I will go to the Gentiles". **(Acts 18:5-6)**

This argument was strengthened because they insisted on denying the LORD's Resurrection and rejected the name of Jesus. They also blasphemed His death on the cross.

The Gospel of John says: **"He came unto his own, and his own received him not. But as many as received him, to them gave He power to become the sons of God even to that believe on his name:"** **(John 1:11-12)**

There is a heresy that upholds the belief that Jesus never died on the cross that He was revived by the disciples. This is a heresy from the Gentiles because they have a reasonable doubt that God the Father would raise a man from the dead.

"And when they heard of the Resurrection of the dead, some mocked: and others said, we will hear thee.
again, of this matter" **(Acts 17:32)** This is the response which the Athenians day to Paul when he preached the Gospel of the Resurrection of Jesus

Christ onto them.

The apostle Paul told the Corinthian church the following:

"And that he was seen of Cephas, then of the Twelve: After that, he was seen of above five hundred brethren at once, of whom the greater part remains unto this present, but some have fallen asleep. After that, he was seen by James then of all the apostles. And last of all he was seen of me also, as of one born out of due time. "(1 Corinthians 15:5 – 8)

Jesus never operated in secret. He never kept anything hidden from His disciples. They knew what kind of death He would face, and by whom. He knew that he would meet them in Jerusalem in the Upper Room after His Resurrection for final instructions in their ministry *"But after I am risen, I will go before you in Galilee"* (Mark 14:28)

So many believed that Christ never returned to do any of the things that Scripture say he did, mainly to meet with His disciples in the Upper Room. This heresy is preached by some Christian believers!

This is very sad, but very true!

The Jews also contend that Jesus never met with the apostles and disciples anywhere after his Resurrection. Anyway, we can certainly understand why the Jews say such things, because they have so much to reject and deny about the Christ, our LORD Jesus. But can we understand why Christians say the same things on this matter? This is a hard question to answer........

Let's be established in our faith, our faith is in the Gospel. If we do not know this fact, then we will always contend about the Gospel of Christ, which gives pleasure to the devil! Amen! The prophet Isaiah tells us: *"If ye will not believe, surely ye shall not be established."* (Isaiah 7:9)

They argue that Jesus told Mary not to touch Him when she met Him in the garden, after His Resurrection. Their argument is that no one else would have been able to touch Him, or even talk with Him. So again, they say that the apostles are lying about Jesus being with them in the Upper Room. But we all know that the LORD told Mary to tell the disciples to meet Him in Galilee. *"And entering into the sepulcher, they saw a young man sitting on the right side, clothed in a long white garment: and they were affrighted."* (Mark 16:5)

They all met in the Upper Room because the LORD Jesus instructed them to meet Him in Galilee upon His Resurrection. He had to give them more instructions about the task that lay ahead in the ministry. They had to be prepared to face confrontation ahead, and how to meet with the Holy Spirit, and what they should expect from the Holy Spirit. They were instructed how to perform in the Holy Spirit's movement for the church. They had to be taught how to meet the Holy Spirit!

Today ministers are not interested to know how to meet the Holy Spirit. This introduction has not happened to many yet, because of their stubbornness! Some ministers do not care about the outpouring of anointing in their ministries. There's no power to preach the Word!

The element of the LORD's ascension is still a matter of disputation on both sides. They dispute that the Gospel of John records that Jesus gave the commission to Peter, as the first pastor of the church, and then immediately ascended into heaven.

They contend that the Gospel of John does not say that Jesus went to the Upper Room with the disciples. Many of them dispute Epistles of Acts of the Apostles, as a thesis to Paul's friend Theophilus. Let's say that scholars dispute the written Word of God and get away with it!

But the child of God believes in the written Word of God, which is the Holy Bible.

This is the Holy Scriptures given to us from God, the Father, through the inspiration of the Holy Spirit! Amen!

The child of God meditates upon the Word in the Spirit. A child of God seeks the understanding of the Word in the powerful anointing of the Holy Spirit. Amen!

"All scripture is given by inspiration of God, and profitable for doctrine, for reproof, for correction, for instruction in righteousness: That the man of God may be perfect, thoroughly furnished unto all good works." (2 Timothy 3:16, 17)

1. The record of all manifestations of our LORD Jesus is to solidify the faith of all the believers, who saw nothing, heard nothing, and yet believed with all their heart. We are blessed in the Lord Jesus. Hallelujah!

"Neither pray I for these alone, but for them also which shall believe on me through their Word." (John 17:20)

2. All manifestations were first decreed by the Father. They were given to the Apostles by the Lord Jesus. Then they were signified by the Holy Spirit.

Jesus said onto the Father:" For I have given unto them the Words which thou gavest me; and they have received them and have known surely that I came out

---

from thee, and they have believed that thou didst send me."
(John 17:8)

3. All manifestations, and revelations from the Father are first given to the ministers of Christ to the edification of the Body of Christ. *"Surely the LORD GOD will do nothing, but He revealeth His secret unto His servants the prophets."* (Amos 3:7)

"And for their sakes I sanctify myself, that they also might be sanctified through the truth. [20] Neither pray I for these alone, but for them also which shall believe on me through their Word;" (John 17:19-20)

4. The Lord Jesus gives ministers revelations through the power of the Holy Spirit. These revelations are given according to will of the Father for the edification of the church!

The apostle Paul said:*" Now we have received, not the spirit of the world, but the spirit which is of God; that we might know the things that are freely given to us by God. For who hath known the mind of the Lord, that he may instruct him? But we have the mind of Christ."* (1 Corinthians 2:12-16)

- Therefore, the spiritual things of God, the Father, must always be the imminent factor of faith of the Body of Christ.
- All ministers must be of the one accord with the Gospel of the Lord (according to their calling).
- We must never labor within the context of tradition and man-made philosophies, but rather in the Word of God.

This Word within our Spirit must be the 'Rhema Word', which we have received within our Spirit from prayerfully studying the Word of God, and seeking the wisdom from God to understand His Word and His purpose in our lives.

We seek the Holy Spirit's guidance for all revelations in the mysteries of the Word, that will bring us into the knowledge of the truth.

Remember the devil's deceitful statement *"And the serpent said unto the woman, Ye shall not surely die"*

(Genesis 3: 4) **But the LORD God had said unto Adam:** *"Thou shalt surely die.* (Genesis 2:17b)

One thing that is so deceitful in all that we have said so far is the way ministers play with the WORD of God. They try to convince the congregation that the Lord God does not punish people as it says in the Word. They believe that by softening messages, they will gain more people in their churches. They portray the LORD as a weakling, and as a beggar, an identification that they call: 'a loving LORD'.

They evade the truth. They do not want to teach about the fury of the LORD Jesus Christ, the Righteous Judge. They say that people are scared to listen to this type of preaching. It is our duty as ministers to teach the congregations about the consequences of disobedience to the will of God.

And the people shall be blessed tremendously!

"Then said Jesus to those Jews which believed on him, If ye continue in my Word, then are ye my disciples indeed, And ye shall know the truth, and the truth

shall make you free". (John 8:31,32)

So let us rightly divide the Word of truth. We are soldiers on the battlefield for Christ. Our labor and ministry shall speak for itself.

The Apostle Peter said: *"For it had been better for them not to have known the way of righteousness, than, after they have known it, to turn from the holy commandment delivered unto them."* (2 Peter 2:21)

"But it is happened unto them according to the true proverb, The dog is turned to his own vomit again; and the sow that was washed to her wallowing in the mire." (2 Peter 2:22)

My brothers and sisters in Christ: Let's stop living in the devil's deceit, but rather live in the Word of Jesus Christ.

The devil has no word!

"But the Word of God does not return void, but it shall

*accomplish that which it pleases the LORD God, and it
shall prosper in the saying whereto He sends it.*
"(Isaiah 53:11)

This devil's deceit has set man backward in His
purpose toward God. This deceit has brought about
sin, disobedience, destruction, and worst of all death.
This is the consequence of not rightly dividing the
Word of truth to congregations. Remember always:
Adam shunned the truth, believing that the LORD God
would not fulfill His Word to Him: *"Thou shalt surely
die."* (Genesis 2:17)

This disobedience has caused us our spiritual and
heavenly life in God because it gave us mortality. We
had lost for a season the immortal soul that was so
freely given to us. Jesus came back to give back our
immortal souls at the Resurrection on the day of
redemption. Let us not lose it again in the second
death.

For Revelation said:" *Blessed and holy is He that hath
part of the first Resurrection on such the day second
death hath no power, but they shall be priests of God*

and of Christ and shall reign with him a thousand years." (Revelation 20:6)

We cannot hide from the truth in the Word of God.

We were created for God's pleasure. We are created in God's image and likeness. Jesus through the Holy Spirit has made us God's spiritual children again. For we are born again in the Holy Spirit. God, the Father gave man dominion over all the earth. Once again, we are the partakers of these great promises, because Jesus died on the cross and has redeemed us to the Father. We are able to claim these privileges before the throne of the Father, through the promises in His Word because we come to God's throne of grace boldly. This is what the cleansing blood of Jesus has done for us; before the Father, we can cry 'Abba Father' in Jesus' name!

The LORD God made woman with the same privilege, to share in the fulness of the purpose of the Father's creation. (Genesis 1:26)

The time has come for us to break away from the devil and believe God. Too long have we played the game of deceit and truth. But we must live for truth, Jesus died for the truth. Sin has no more authority over us. Sin will have no authority again in our lives. Once we have been born again in the Holy Spirit and have tasted the goodness of God, we must never return to our sinful ways.

We must not return to our vomit, which is to deceive the congregation about the issues of sin! Praise you Holy Spirit! *"O taste and see that the Lord is good: blessed is the man that trusteth in Him."* (Psalms 34:8) The power of the
Resurrection of Christ must take hold of our lives in Christ!

Our faith is alive, not dead!

We believe therefore we have spoken! Glory to God!

"We having the same Spirit of faith, according as it is written, I believe, and therefore have I spoken; we also believe, and therefore speak" (2 Corinthians 4:13) *"I believed, therefore have I spoken: I was greatly afflicted."* (Psalms 116:10)

The apostle Paul said to those who refuse to live in the power Of the Resurrection of Christ the following Words:" O *death, where is thy sting? O grave, where is thy victory? The sting of death is sin; and the strength of sin is the law, but thanks be to God, which giveth us the victory through our LORD Jesus Christ* (1 Corinthians 15:55 – 57)

Jesus Christ is our victory. Amen*! "And God hath both raised up the Lord and will also raise us up by his own power."* (1 Corinthians 6:14)

Jesus had many witnesses in His Resurrection:" *And that he was seen of Cephas, then of the Twelve: After that, he was seen of above five hundred brethren at once: of whom the greater part remain unto this present, but some are fallen asleep."* (1 Corinthians 15:5,6)

Jesus went to Hell and took the keys of Hell and death from the devil. (Revelation 1:18) *"He that descended is the same also, that ascended up far above all heavens, that he might fill all things".* (Ephesians 4:10)

The Father called Him from the grave, and from hell. *"But we see Jesus, who was made a little lower than the angels for the suffering of death, crowned with glory and honor; that He by the grace of God should taste death for every man. "*(Hebrews 2:9)

"There is no intention about this written Word for the child of God. We know that our Lord is alive and well at the right hand of the Father! He is our High Priest before the Father strong for us! Amen!

Paul said to the Galatians the following: *"Christ hath redeemed us from the curse of the law, being made a curse for us: for it is written, cursed is everyone that hangeth on a tree: That the blessing of Abraham might come on the Gentiles through Jesus Christ: that we might receive the promise of the Spirit through faith."* (Galatians 3:13, 14)

These are the controversial issues that concern Christ; they make us ask ourselves questions like these:
1. Are the Jews saying that the Messiah should not have died on the cross to redeem the whole world?
2. Should He come to them only?

Let's consider these things…
Remember the LORD God had given them a great responsibility to the world, they were called to be the Royal priesthood, to carry the Word of God for the edification of mankind.

"Now therefore, if ye will obey my voice indeed, and keep my covenant, then ye shall be a peculiar treasure unto me above all people: for all the earth is mine: And ye shall be unto me a kingdom of priests, and a holy nation. These are the words which thou shalt speak unto the children of Israel." (Exodus 19:5,6) The Law of the LORD God was given unto them that they might teach the world.

The ways of God, the Father, in the earth, through the LORD, The Lord God was also made known unto them through Moses. (Exodus 34:5,6)

These are the seven ways of God, the Father on the earth. They are His seven Spirits that rule the earth through the Lord God, Jesus Christ:

"And I beheld, and, lo, in the midst of the throne and of the four beasts, and in the midst of the elders, stood a Lamb as it had been slain, having seven horns and seven eyes, which are the seven Spirits of God sent forth into all the earth. (Revelations 5:6)

Therefore, the first Spirit, stands in the name of:
1. The LORD, the LORD God. Because it is through the LORD God. God, the Son, these ways are executed throughout the earth.
2. Merciful
3. Gracious
4. Long-suffering
5. Abundant in goodness AND truth
6. Keeping mercy for thousands, forgiving inequity and
transgression and sin, and will by no means clear the guilty.
7. Visiting the iniquity of the fathers upon the children and upon the children's children onto the third and
fourth generation (Exodus 34:5 -7)

The world should have been taught this truth.

But many ministries would not consider this of any importance to the congregation.

The apostle Paul said: *"For when for the time ye ought to be teachers, ye have need that one teach you again which be the first principles of the oracles of God; and are become such as have need of milk, and not of strong meat."* (Hebrews 5:12*)*

" Behold I stand at the door and knock"
(Revelation 3:20)

Chapter 4:
The Beast That Rises Up Out of the Sea

"And I stood upon the sand of the sea, and saw a beast rise up out of the sea, having seven heads and ten horns, and upon his horns ten crowns, and upon his heads the name of blasphemy." (Revelation 13:1)

THE POWER OF THE NAME OF JESUS:

My brothers and sisters in Christ the first pattern of this revelation about the beast is the identity of the beast. The identity of the beast is that he rises up out of the sea. The beast rises up out of the Nation of Israel.

Apostle John said I stood on the sand of the sea. This term is taken from the prophecies to Abraham concerning the number of children promised to him:

1. *"That in blessing I will bless thee and in multiplying I will multiply thy seed as the stars of heaven and of the sand which is on*

the seashore; and thy seed shall possess the gate of his enemies."(Genesis 22:17)

2. Isaiah said the following: **"For though thy people Israel be as the sand of the sea, yet a remnant of them shall return: the consumption decreed shall overflow with righteousness."** (Isaiah 10: 22) (Romans 9:27)

3. Hosea said **"Yet the number of the children of Israel shall be as the sand of the sea, which cannot be measured nor numbered; and it shall come to pass, that in the place where it was said unto them, Ye are not my people, there it shall be said unto them, Ye are the sons of the living God."** (Hosea 1:10) (Romans: 9:27)

4. Paul spoke to the Hebrew church the following **"Therefore sprang there even of one, and him as good as dead, so many as the stars of the sky in multitude, and as the sand which is by the sea shore innumerable."** (Hebrews 11:12)

The beast has seven heads and ten horns in upon his horns ten crowns and upon his head name of blasphemy. **(Revelations 13:1)**

These seven heads represent the seven churches, to which the LORD Jesus sends his final prophecy in messages. Because the ministry of the beast is established within the ministry of the church of Christ. This is the spotted ministry spoken of by Paul, Peter, John, and Jude.

These are the seven churches:
1. The church at Ephesus
2. The church at Smyrna
3. The church at Pergamos
4. The church at Philadelphia
5. The church at Sardis
6. The church at Thyatira
7. The church at Laodicea **(Revelations 1:11)**

The seven churches represent the whole Body of Christ. These messages then were sent to all churches in the Body of Christ. Because the number seven is the number of completion in the Scriptures. It is the number of perfection.

The LORD Jesus was commissioned by the Father to give His final prophecy to all those that are His in the earth. HIS CHURCH!

The number seven represents all who are the body of Christ and are called by his name! The Christian church!

The revelation of the beast rising up out of the nation of Israel is the result of many elders of the Jews, who came into the Body of Christ, at the beginning of the organization of the church. These elders insisted they continue fulfilling the law.

The Pharisees insisted that the Gentile believers continue to observe the law. **(Acts 15:5,6)**
The Sadducees, who were converted into Christianity, continued their argument against the Resurrection of Jesus. Paul said of this argument:

"Now if Christ be preached that he rose from the dead, how say some among you that there is no

Resurrection of the dead? But if there be no Resurrection of the dead, then is Christ not risen: And if Christ be not risen, then is our preaching vain, and your faith is also vain. (1 Corinthians 15:12 – 14)

This is why this counsel of the apostle was so important, for the continuation of the work for the church. **(Acts 15: 1 – 29)**

"But there rose up certain sect of the Pharisees which believed, saying, that it was needful to circumcise them, and to command them to keep the law of Moses. And the apostles and elders came together to consider this matter. (Acts 15:5 – 6)

This is what the apostles and elders agreed on in that counsel:

- That we worship the first day of the week.

- That we abstain from meat offered to idols and from any other type of sacrificial offering *(and rituals, that is not of the commandment of Christ).*

- That Gentiles in the faith of Christ do not keep the Law of Moses. Jesus was crucified to fulfill the law.

- That we are the faith of non-circumcision.**(Acts 15:1-29).**

This was the beginning of manifestations of the controversies to the Gospel of Christ, by Jews and Gentiles, who questioned the veracity of the principles of the Christian faith. For the contention of these controversies were already infiltrated in many of the churches, by Jews and Gentiles, who were elders of the churches.
Jesus spoke to the seven pastors in the seven churches about the way in which they administered the Gospel to the Body.

Each message to each church describes a church that is in operation today! Several pastors are administering their congregation contrary to the will of Jesus Christ, And Jesus continues to send them the same message. Pastors continuously pretend that they have no understanding about anything the Lord said in his seven messages to the seven churches.

So many pastors do not study this prophecy of Revelation, because it does not excite them. So many ministries have no idea of what the Holy Spirit is saying to the church today! Therefore the trend and movement of the Holy Spirit in the church today is passing their ministries by.....

Many pastors and ministers are out of tune with the Holy Spirit. They must acknowledge the execution of God's Word in the lives of all believers. Let's get involved with the trend of the Holy Spirit in the church today! .

Whenever a church is undecided about the execution of God's Word in the lives of the believers, false teachers take over, and the result of this action is a very cold church! There will be no power in the 'preaching' word. No power then in this spoken word is evidence of the absence of the Holy Spirit. The absence of the Holy Spirit means no anointing in the ministry!

The Lord Jesus is not pleased with this annoying behavior in His church!

People of God, wake up to the move of the Holy Spirit before it is too late!

The beast has ten horns and upon his horns ten crowns:

The ten horns are the ten controversial issues that have haunted the church from the beginning. Therefore, the number ten represents the symbolic number of denominations that have derived from these controversies! These ten horns have ten crowns: A Crown represents ministry. For the reward of the servant of Christ, or minister is a CROWN. Therefore, these are the ministries who are ordained to operate the denominations that represent the church of Christ in the earth.

Remember, Jesus wears a golden crown in heaven. He is our High Priest before the Father! They crucified Jesus with a crown of thorns to mock Him. But they were actually distinguishing Him on the cross between the two thieves because this was the way in which the angels would recognize Jesus on the cross.

All the high priests of the Levitical priesthood wear a crown. Moses was commanded to make the crown for Aaron. **(Exodus 29:6)**

Job, the Melchizedek high priest, wore a crown *"**He hath stripped me of my glory and taken the crown from my head.**" (Job 19:9)*

These are the Ten Outstanding Controversies in the Church

The seven heads represent the seven churches to whom Jesus spoke. These theologies contradict and defile the principles of the Gospel These are deep rooted beliefs that are used to blaspheme the name of Jesus. Paul said of these blasphemies the following:" ***They are all gone out of the way, they are together become unprofitable; there is none that doeth good, no, not one. Their throat is an open sepulcher; with their tongues they have used deceit;***

the poison of asps is under their lips Whose mouth is full of cursing and bitterness: **(Romans 3:12-14)**

This blasphemous ministry is called the spotted ministry because it is spotted like a leopard. Because the beast is described as a leopard.

Jesus Christ our LORD has stripes not spots!

And ***"by His stripes we are healed."*** **(Isaiah 53:5) (1 Peter 2:24)**

Not by the spots of Jesus we are healed!
Jesus has no spots!
Jesus has stripes from the Romans' whips!

Lest we forget that:" Spots represent the lies that are taught about Christ and the Gospel!" by very cunning individuals.

Jude speaks about the infiltrated ministry and says ***"These are spots in your feasts of charity, when they feast with you, feeding themselves without fear: clouds they are without water, carried about of*** *winds; trees whose fruit withered, without fruit, twice dead, plucked up by the roots;"* (Jude: verse 12)

The feet of the beast:

"And his feet were like the feet of a bear,"

The feet of these ministers are for deceit and destruction. They are swift to devour the sheepfold of the LORD. This is what the feet of a bear does: devour, destroys, and kills.

Paul said to the Roman church the following about them: ***"Their feet are swift to shed blood"*** **(Romans 3:15)**

But feet of one who preaches the Gospel of salvation is described in the following way: Isaiah tells us:*" **How beautiful upon the mountains are the feet of him that bringeth good tidings, that publisheth peace; that bringeth good tidings of good, that publisheth salvation; that saith unto Zion, Thy God reigneth!"** **(Isaiah 52:7)**

The prophet Nahum said:*" **Behold upon the mountains the feet of him that bringeth good tidings, that publisheth peace!." (Nahum 1:15a)***

Paul said again in regard to this issue **"How then shall they call on him in whom they have not believed? and how shall they believe in him of whom they have not heard? and how shall they hear without a preacher?" (Romans 10:14,15)**

We also know from Ephesians: **"And your feet shod with the preparation of the Gospel of peace;" (Ephesians 6:15)**

Revelation tells us **"Here is wisdom. Let him that hath understanding count the number of the beast: for it is the number of a man; and his number is Six hundred threescore and six. (Revelation 13:18)**

This is 666:

The first (Six) represents the image of the beast

The number (Six) represents man. Because man was made on the sixth day of the creation. **(Genesis 1:27-31)**

The Word of God calls any man, especially a servant of the LORD, who is foolish, and have no spiritual understanding, and is lacking a life:

1. A Fool: ***"The fool hath said in his heart, There is no God. They are corrupt, they have done abominable works, there is none that doeth good."*** (Psalm 14:1)

2. A beast: David's confession to the LORD. ***"So foolish was I, and ignorant: I was as a beast before thee"*** *(Psalms 73:22)*

3. Brutish: Again, the psalmist said: ***"A brutish man knoweth not; neither doth a fool understand this."*** (Psalms 92:6)***"*** *For the pastors are become brutish, and have not sought the LORD:"* (Jeremiah 10:21a)

The pastors had no prayer life, therefore no communication with the Holy Spirit.

"Nevertheless man being in honor abideth not: he is like the beasts that perish. (Psalm 49:12)

He who does not obey the Words of the LORD is like the beast that perishes. Jesus said*: "If ye abide in me, and my Words abide in you, ye shall ask what ye will, and it shall be done unto you." (John 15:7) "Man that is in honor, and understandeth not, is like the beasts that perish." (Psalms 49:20)*
A man that understands nothing about the Word of the Lord is like the beast that perishes!

"Evil men understand not judgment: but they that seek the Lᴏʀᴅ understand all things. (Proverbs 28:5)
When we seek the LORD, the Holy Spirit, in prayer, we are able to understand all things. This knowledgeable and educated priesthood has confused the message of Christ. This organization has had its appointed leader down through the ages. The leader is a minister who stands as a traitor to the cause of Christ, a son of perdition empowered by Satan to disrupt the Gospel. **(2 Thessalonians 2:3-12)**

The second (Six) represents the name of the beast.

This is the name that the beast gives himself. The activity is a manifestation of the type of personality and character that the beast portrays before people, this personality testifies to the great miracle that happened to one of the heads of the beast.

This head survived a deadly wound of a sword, and the survival is a marvel to the world who do not know the truth about Jesus' death. *"And they worshiped the dragon which gave power unto the beast: and they worshiped the beast, saying, Who is like unto the beast? Who is able to make war with him?"* (Revelation 13:4) *"Saying to them that dwell on the earth, that they should make an image to the beast, which had the wound by a sword, and did live."* (Revelation 13:14b)

Jesus wants us against these days of false prophets and false Christs: *"For there shall arise false Christs, and false prophets, and shall shew great signs and wonders; insomuch that, if it were possible, they shall deceive the very elect."* (Matthew 24:24) This testimony of the beast is to demonstrate that Jesus was not resurrected from the dead. Because Jesus could not have died on the cross; he was revived by his disciples.

This means that no man dies and rises again!

The world who rejects Christ accepts the testimony of the beast.

The LORD Jesus said: ***"Then if any man shall say unto you, Lo, here is Christ, or there; believe it not."*** **(Matthew 24:23) *"For false Christs and false prophets shall rise, and shall shew signs and wonders, to seduce, if it were possible, even the elect."* (Mark 13:22) *"Here is wisdom. Let him that hath understanding count the number of the beast: for it is the number of a man; and his number is Six hundred threescore and six."* (Revelations 13:18)**

Brothers and sisters in Christ: we are living in the time of the ten virgins. We are entering into history's darkest hour, the midnight hour, which Jesus spoke about!

It is true that the Gospel is preached all over the world like never before, but it is also true that evil is rampant everywhere, even in the Body of Christ. Ministers are deceiving congregations everywhere with false teachings.

Let's consider Noah and the Word of the LORD: While Noah preached the Word of prophecy that was commissioned unto him for the people of God, concerning the flood he had to have prayed fervently to the LORD God to give him understanding on how to discern the Lord's movement. This movement of the Lord God is the gradual steps in which the Lord fulfills His prophetic Word, by allowing man time for repentance.

Remember always: that God, the Father desires that no man should perish, but all should have eternal life.

The movement of the LORD will come with the manifestations of:

- Famine
- Diseases
- War
- Crimes
- Violence
- Strange weather patterns

- A great thirst for the Word of God among all people, which brings a great revival in the earth.

There are Watchers of the earth through which these movements are manifested as recorded in **(Zechariah 6:1 – 9)** *"These are the four spirits of heaven, which go forth from standing before the Lord of all the earth."*

- The white horse rider has a crown and a bow. He sets out to conquer. **(Revelation 6: 2)**

- The crown represents ministry; the bow is the preaching of the Word, which pierces the heart of the believers to convict them.

- The red horse rider has a great sword that made war in the earth. **(Revelation 6:4)**

- The black horse rider has a scale. Hebrews famous in the earth. **(Revelation 6:6)**

- The pale gray horse represents death and sickness in the earth. **(Revelation 6:8)**

The movement of the Lord is always according to the prophetic Word of the Lord to His servants. For the Word of God will accomplish that which He sends it out to accomplish, and it will be fulfilled in the time in which God the Father has set for it to come to pass.

As it is written in Isaiah *"So shall my word be that goeth forth out of my mouth: it shall not return unto me void, but it shall accomplish that which I please, and it shall prosper in the thing whereto I sent it.* "(Isaiah 55:11)** The spiritual man will discern the signs of the time and will pray for wisdom and understanding.

Noah also prayed for wisdom to accomplish a task set before him by the Lord God and the Lord gave him the wisdom and understanding to make the ark, and to preach to the people righteously. This is why Noah and his family were saved and entered into the ark because he sought the wisdom of the LORD in fervent prayer to do the Lord's work according to his will. Peter spoke of Noah and said: *"And spared not the old world, but saved Noah the eighth person, a preacher of righteousness, bringing in the flood upon the world of the ungodly;"* (2 Peter 2:5)

This is the time of the movement of the Lord God, Jesus Christ, through the power of the Holy Spirit in the church for his time is near! Let us therefore pray for the understanding and wisdom of this movement, and like Noah, we will be able to preach Words of righteousness to God's people.

Another movement of the Lord Jesus today is the way time passes quickly. Jesus has already told us to look out for this evidence ***"And except those days should be shortened, there should no flesh be saved: but for the elect's sake those days shall be shortened."*** **(Matthew 24:22)** Jesus speaks about the darkest hour in man's existence where he said:***" Then shall the kingdom of heaven be likened unto ten virgins, who took their lamps, and went forth to meet the bridegroom."*** **(Matthew 25:1)** *He illustrates the seriousness of the times in which all these things will be openly manifested to all believers.*

Although this priesthood and his activities have existed since the foundation of the church they have always operated in disguise, and fooled many believers who are stubborn, and unwilling to listen to the warning .: ***"Wherefore come out from among them, and be ye separate, saith the Lord, and touch not the unclean thing; and I will receive you."*(2 Corinthians 6:17)**

They have successfully concealed their true determination, and they have fooled the crowds. Jesus said, ***"For nothing is secret, that shall not be made manifest; neither anything hidden, that shall not be known and come abroad. Take heed therefore how ye hear: for whosoever hath, to him shall be given; and whosoever hath not, from him shall be taken even that which he seemeth to have."* (Luke 8:17,18)**

The third (Six) represents the mark of the beast.

The mark of the beast is his doctrine. This doctrine is the foundation on which his religion stands. The miracle of the survival of his head which was wounded by the sword:

The head which was wounded by the sword speaks of one of the beastly ministries wounded almost to death by a sword. This was a time of drastic disputation in the Word of God. A contention that was

so grievous it brought ward to the ministry of Christ."
*And he opened his mouth in blasphemy against God,
to blaspheme his name, and his tabernacle, and
them that dwell in heaven. And it was given unto
him to make war with the saints, and to overcome
them: and power was given him over all kinds,
tongues, and nations."* (Revelation 13:6,7)

The "Swords" represents two meanings:

- The Word of God

- The weapon on war

The Word is spoken of in both meanings in verses six and seven.

Verse speaks of the blasphemy he speaks about the Word of God:

- **"And he opened his mouth in blasphemy against God;**

- **To blaspheme his name**

- **And his tabernacle**

- **And them that dwell in heaven"**

The beast blasphemed against the scriptures. He blasphemed against the name of Jesus. He blasphemed against the church, and against the saints of God. **(Revelation 13:6)**

The apostle Paul said:" ***For the Word of God is quick, and powerful, and sharper than any two-edged sword, piercing even to the dividing asunder of soul and spirit, and of the joints and marrow, and is a discerner of the thoughts and intents of the heart."*** **(Hebrews 4:12)**

The second meaning to the Word "sword" is quite clear in verse seven: ***"And it was given unto him to make war with the saints, and to overcome them: and power was given him over all kinds, tongues, and nations."*** **(Revelation 13:7)**

Devastation, divisions, and war, within the Body of Christ, weakened the wounded head for a period of time. So, this ministry went through drastic transformation and lost a great number of its followers. But in the course of time, through much bribery and manipulation, this particular head was able to rise again.

This time stronger in its misconceptions and misleading information, about the Gospel and scriptures. This head was stronger and more determined to execute its mission to destroy the image of Christ. This surviving head of the beast arose with an image of power and prestige among nations who do know the LORD Jesus.

This particular head has a victorious personality and is considered above all others who ridicule the Gospel of Christ.

Therefore, this particular head of the beast has its own image in Christ's ministry. ***"And all that dwell upon the earth shall worship him, whose names are not written in the book of life of the Lamb slain from the foundation of the world."*** (Revelation 13:8)

"Behold I stand at the door and knock"
(Revelations 3:20)

Chapter 5:

The Ten Fundamental Controversies

The ten fundamental controversies represent the ten horns of the beast that rise up out of the sea *"And I stood upon the sand of the sea, and saw a beast rise up out of the sea, having seven heads and ten horns, and upon his horns ten crowns, and upon his heads the name of blasphemy."* (Revelation 13:1)

These ten fundamental controversies are the ten horns of the beast that rises up out of the sea. These are the fundamental controversies of the testimony of Christ from the very foundation for the church:

1. **The Denial of His Second Coming**
   - *"Knowing this first, that there shall come in the last days scoffers, walking after their own lusts, [4] And saying, where is the promise of his coming? For since the Fathers fell asleep, all things continue as they were from the beginning of the creation.* (2 Peter 3:3,4)

2. **The Denial that Jesus is the Christ.**
    - *"Whosoever denieth the Son, the same hath not the Father: he that acknowledgeth the Son hath the Father also. "(1 John 2:23)*

    - *"Little children, it is the last time: and as ye have heard that antichrist shall come, even now are there many antichrists; whereby we know that it is the last time. They went out from us, but they were not of us; for if they had been of us, they would no doubt have continued with us: but they went out, that they might be made manifest that they were not all of us. (1 John 2:18-19)*

3. **The Denial of the Resurrection of the saints at the Coming of the Lord Jesus.**
    - *"Who concerning the truth have erred, saying that the Resurrection*

> ***is past already; and overthrow the
> faith of some. "(2 Timothy 2:18)***

4. **The Denial that Jesus Christ has come in the flesh.**
   - ***"And every spirit that confesseth not that Jesus Christ has come in the flesh is not of God: and this is that spirit of antichrist, whereof ye have heard that it should come; and even now already is it in the world. (1 John 4:3)***

5. **The Denial of the Resurrection of Christ**
   - ***"Now if Christ be preached that he rose from the dead, how say some among you that there is no Resurrection of the dead? But if there be no Resurrection of the dead, then is Christ not risen: And if Christ be not risen, then is our preaching vain, and your faith is also vain " (1 Corinthians 15:12-14)***

6. **The Justification by Law**

- ***Paul, an apostle, (not of men, neither by man, but by Jesus Christ, and God the Father, who raised him from the dead;)"** (Galatians 1:1)*

- ***"For by grace are ye saved through faith; and that not of yourselves: it is the gift of God: Not of works, lest any man should boast."** (Ephesians 2:8,9)*

7. **The Controversy of Worshiping Angels in the Church**
   - ***"Let no man beguile you of your reward in a voluntary humility and worshiping of angels, intruding into those things which he hath not seen, vainly puffed up by his fleshly mind, "**(Colossians 2:18)*

8. **Witchcraft within the Ministry of Christ**
   - False prophets, false christs, false leaders and strange theologians infiltrating the Gospel. Philosophy and mythology taking the place of

the Gospel. The Lord's message to the church at Pergamos: ***"But I have a few things against thee, because thou hast there them that hold the doctrine of Balaam, who taught Balac to cast a stumbling block before the children of Israel, to eat things sacrificed unto idols, and to commit fornication."*** **(Revelation 2:14)**

- The church at Thyatira had the same message on the same subject for the Pastor had allowed a prophetess with the spirit of Jezebel to teach and subject the ministers to the knowledge of witchcraft and fornication and to eat meat sacrificed unto idols. **(Revelation 2:20-23)**

9. The Controversy of the Jews
- Jesus is not the Messiah.
- The controversy of the birth of our Lord

- The Jews believe that Jesus' body was stolen from the tomb by His disciples
- They reject the name of Jesus.
- A commandment for all Christians **(1 John 3:23)**

10. The Authority of Jesus in the Church: That Jesus is the Head of the Church, not 666!

- They question the Holy Spirit.
- They deny the power of the Holy Spirit.

- They ignore Him in all their worship.

- They say that all miracles and manifestations of the power of the Holy Spirit are past, that this was from the time of the disciples.

- They deny speaking in tongues, which the Holy Spirit gives us utterance, to speak through His anointing.

"Behold I stand at the door and knock."
(Revelation 3:20)

Chapter 6:

The Description of the Beast

"The beast which I saw was like unto a leopard, and his feet were as the feet of a bear, and his mouth as the mouth of a lion: And the dragon gave him his power, and his seat, and great authority. And she, being with child cried, travailing in birth, and pained to be delivered." (Revelation 13:2)

Let's consider this description of the beast:

1. The beast was like a leopard. A leopard is a spotted beast:

- The ministry of the beast is called the ministry, and Jude called them spots in the feasts of the real ministers, *"And shall receive the reward of unrighteousness, as they count it pleasure to riot in the day time. Spots they are and blemishes, sporting themselves with their own deceiving while they feast with you;"(Jude, verse 12a)*

- Peter called them: ***"But these, as natural brute beasts, made to be taken and destroyed, speak evil of the things that they understand not; and shall utterly perish in their own corruption; "(2 Peter 2:12)***

2. His feet like a bear:
   - ***"Their feet are swift to shed blood (Romans 3:15)***
   - ***"For of this sort are they which creep into houses, and lead captive silly women laden with sins, led away with divers lusts, Ever learning, and never able to come to the knowledge of the truth (2 Timothy 3:6,7)***

3. And his mouth as the mouth of a lion:
   - ***"Whose mouth is full of cursing and bitterness: "(Romans 3:14)***

4. The dragon gave him his power:

   - ***"Even him, whose coming is after the working of Satan with all power and signs and lying wonders," (2 Thessalonians 2:9)***

5. And his seat:

> ***"I know thy works, and where thou dwellest, even where Satan's seat is:."*** **(Revelations 2:13a)**

6. And great authority

- ***"Who opposeth himself above all that are called God, or that is worshiped so that he as God sitteth in the temple of God shewing himself that he is God."*** **(2 Thessalonians 2:4)**
- The son of perdition **(2 Thessalonians 2:3b)**
- Judas was also called the son of perdition by the LORD Jesus. ***"While I was with them in the world, I kept them in thy name: those that thou gavest me I have kept, and none of them is lost, but the son of perdition; that the scripture might be fulfilled."*** **(John 17:12)**
- He betrayed the LORD.

Likewise, this apostate ministry, and its leaders are traitors to the cause of Jesus, the Christ of God! They are traitors to the fundamental principles of the

Gospel. These ministers possess the spirit of Judas which is the spirit of treason.

They are walking in the light of the church at Thyatira. This church had the spirit of Jezebel.
"Notwithstanding I have a few things against thee, because thou sufferest that woman Jezebel, which calleth herself a prophetess, to teach and to seduce my servants to commit fornication, and to eat things sacrificed unto idols." **(Revelation 2:20)**

Jezebel was the wicked queen that ruled Israel with her husband Ahab during the lifetime of Elijah the prophet. Ahab was a weakling and very disobedient to the LORD God of Israel. He obeyed his wife rather than the LORD God's commandments. She was the high priestess to their god, Baal. She was a woman full of idolatry and witchcraft. **(1 Kings 21:1-15)**

This Jezebel spirit is the spirit of witchcraft; it preys on the weakness of unstable ministers who have no praying life, this is no life in the Holy Spirit. These ministers do not say the Word, they are weak and unstable from lack of communication with the Holy Spirit. Ministers such as these cannot say *"Thus saith*

LORD to this congregation." Please pray for them!

This Jezebel spirit is a possessive spirit. It possesses things that are not its own. This possessive spirit has a false appearance. It manipulates everyone who allows the manipulation and deceives the same people into strange doctrines. It is a spirit of hypocrisy. It is a domineering spirit very covetous and capricious. Thank you, Holy Spirit, for revelation knowledge.

This is not a subject concerning women laboring in the ministry as the devil would like us to believe. If we believe this tale, we are yet honoring another one of the devil's wiles. Amen! And we know that all the wiles of the devil are determined to disrupt and undermine the ministry in the church!

Remember that Satan was our accuser before the throne of God, the Father. Therefore, we are told about the way he was cast out of heaven with his angels ***"For the accuser of our brethren is cast down, which accused them before our God Day and night."*** **(Revelation 12:10b)**

How did this happen?

"And there was war in heaven: Michael and his angels fought against the dragon; and the dragon fought and his angels and prevailed not; neither was their place found any more in heaven. And the great dragon was cast out, that old serpent, called the Devil, and Satan, which deceiveth the whole world: he was cast out into the earth, and his angels were cast out with him. (Revelation 12:7-9)

The Lord Jesus told us about his great heavenly victory: *"And he said unto them, I beheld Satan as lightning fall from heaven."* (Luke 10:18) Therefore, the Lord Jesus is teaching us to be aware of vile teachers, such as this one at Thyatira, who is commissioned by the pastor to teach the servants of Christ, about the ministry of the Gospel, and she teaches them instead that which was contrary to the Word of God.

She taught them how to commit fornication. No minister of Christ must be in fornication. The apostle Peter said *"As obedient children, not fashioning yourselves according to the former lusts in your ignorance"* (1 Peter 1:14) The apostle Paul said *"Therefore if any man be in Christ, he is a new*

creature: old things are passed away; behold, all things are become new. (2 Corinthians 5:17)

She taught him how to eat things sacrificed unto idols. This was established in the council of the apostles at the foundation of the church that all believers, especially ministers must not eat anything sacrificed to idols.

"Wherefore my sentence is that we trouble not them which from among the Gentiles are turned to God: But that we write unto them, that they abstain from pollutions of idols, and from fornication, and from things strangled, and from blood." (Acts 15:19,20)

May I say also, that this is very much alive today in many secular churches. They are called the feasts celebration. These feasts are observed to close out of a fast which was dedicated to a certain deity. Sound familiar?

We can go on and on about discrepancies to the Gospel of Christ. But this discussion will have no objective because brethren will continue in disobedience and rebellion until the coming of the LORD Jesus.

This is why Jesus told John the following: ***"Behold, I stand at the door, and knock: if any man hears my voice, and open the door, I will come into him, and will sup with him, and he with me."*** (Revelation 3:20)

The Great Testimony of the Beast:
The victory of the beast in the eyes of the world ***"And I saw one of his heads as it were wounded to death; and his deadly wound was healed: and all the world wondered after the beast."*** (Revelation 13:3)

The organization of the beast derives from the belief of continuing in the law. The apostle Paul addresses the issue concerning **"*saved by grace and not by works :*" He spoke to the Galatians Corinthians and other churches**

"Let no man deceive you by any means: for that day shall not come, except there come a falling away first, and that man of sin be revealed, the son of perdition; Who opposeth and exalteth himself above all that is called God, or that is worshiped; so that he as God sitteth in the temple of God, shewing himself that he is God." (2 Thessalonians 2:3,4)

"And then shall that Wicked be revealed, whom the Lord shall consume with the spirit of His mouth and shall destroy with the brightness of His coming: even him, whose coming is after the working of Satan with all power and signs and lying wonders, and with all deceivableness of unrighteousness in them that perish; because they received not the love of the truth, that they might be saved." (2 Thessalonians 2:8 – 10)

"The nation shall see and be confounded at all their might, they shall lay their hand upon their mouth, their ears shall be deaf." (Micah 7:15 – 16)

Remember the nation of Israel fought with the seven nations that occupied the Promised Land. They were commanded by the LORD God to drive them out, and claim this land of promise to their forefathers Abraham, Isaac, and Jacob. The seven nations were:

1. Canaanites
2. Hittites
3. Amorites
4. Perizzites

5. Hivites
6. Jebusites
7. Gergashites

The nations from far off, such as the inheritance of the children of Esau, the children of Ismael, the inheritance of the children of Lot, etc. ....were confused by the awesome might and wonders of this nation. They were so afraid of the awesome God of Israel

Again, this is true today! For Israel is once again in battle daily, about the division of the land; between them and those who inhabit the land. And once again the nations far off are confused by these conflicts. But yet they are moved greatly by what is happening daily.

"Pray for the peace of Jerusalem." (Psalms 122:6)

The land of Israel is ruled by the sword. Their avenger is the angel of the red horse. Michael, the Archangel. Therefore, they will triumph in all times of war! It is the will of God. Bless you Jesus!

Especially now, for the time has come for a new move of God on the earth!

"And at that time shall Michael stand up, the great prince which standeth for the children of thy people: and there shall be a time of trouble, such as never was since there was a nation even to that same time: and at that time thy people shall be delivered, every one that shall be found written in the book." (Daniel 12:1)

Israel as a nation blasphemes the name of Jesus. They speak these blasphemes with great pride because they believe that this is right in the sight of the LORD God. They feel that this is righteous in the eyes of the God of Abraham, Isaac, and Jacob. But they do not know their LORD God. Because *"He came unto his own, and his own received him not."* **(John 1:11)**

They are a nation of wealth. This is the Word of promise to Abraham, being fulfilled from the LORD. *"That in blessing I will bless thee, and in multiplying I will multiply thy seed as the stars of the heaven, and as the sand which is upon the seashore; and thy seed shall possess the gate of his enemies;"* (Genesis 22:17)

"The Word of the LORD God, in action: *"So shall my Word be that goeth forth out of my mouth: it shall not return unto me void, but it shall accomplish that which I please, and it shall prosper in the thing whereto I sent it."* (Isaiah 55:11)

Therefore, Abraham's children shall be blessed.

We are blessed for we are the spiritual children of Abraham (Galatians 3:14)

That the blessing of Abraham might come to the Gentile through Jesus Christ that we might receive the promise of the Spirit through faith.

They have returned to the Promised Land. Again, the Word of the LORD God in action: *"Thus saith the Lord of hosts; Behold, I will save my people from the east country, and from the west country; And I will bring them, and they shall dwell in the midst of*

Jerusalem: and they shall be my people, and I will be their God, in truth and in righteousness." **(Zechariah 8:7,8)**

The victory is the testimony of the restoration of their Promised Land, and nation.

All Christians who know their LORD and are doing exploits in the name of Jesus recognize that this is the Word of the LORD being fulfilled before our very eyes. They also know that these are the signs of the times of the return of Jesus.

"But the people that do know their God shall be strong, and do exploits. And they that understand among the people shall instruct many: " **(Daniel 11:32,33)**

We are doing exploits in the Word, because we understand the Word, in the anointing of the Holy Spirit. We are moved only by what the Spirit says to the church.

This is the Word of God in our lives!

We study the Word to overcome the wiles of the devil!

Our feet are shod with the preparation of the Gospel. Hallelujah! Amen!

Evidence that this chapter in the book of Revelation speaks of the Jews is the verse. ***"He that leadeth into captivity shall go into captivity; he that killeth with the sword must be killed with the sword. Here is the patience and the faith of the saints"***. **(Revelation 13:10)**

"For they that take the sword shall perish with the sword" **(Matthew 26:32)** ***"The law of the LORD God, is the children Israel."*** **(Exodus 21:12)**

"Behold, I stand at the door and knock"
(Revelations 3:20)

- Minister Glendora Shan Thomas -

- Minister Glendora Shan Thomas -

Chapter 7:

Let's Consider the Following

THE IMAGE OF JESUS
- **The image of Jesus is His identification to the church. This identification is that He is the Anointed One of God, the Father.**
- ***"And said unto them, Thus it is written, and thus it behooved Christ to suffer, and to rise from the dead the third day: And that repentance and remission of sins should be preached in his name among all nations, beginning at Jerusalem." (Luke 24:46, 47)***

JESUS IS TRULY THE CHRIST OF GOD.

- This image of Christ gives us the power to become sons and daughters of God.

THE MARK OF JESUS is His testimony.

- The Gospel is the testimony of Jesus Christ.

This mark is the spirit of prophecy, the angel told John: **"*Worship God for the testimony of Jesus is the spirit of prophecy*" (Revelation 19:10)**

- The testimony of Jesus gives life to the Word of prophecy.

THE POWER IN THE NAME OF JESUS.

- Jesus has the most powerful name in all the universe.
- Jesus told us to call upon His name, in prayer to the Father.
- Jesus said **"*Verily, verily, I say unto you, Whatsoever ye shall ask the Father in my name, he will give it you (John 16:23)***
- **God has given Jesus the name above all names: "That at the**

> **name of Jesus every knee should bow, of things in heaven, and things in the earth and things under the earth; And that every tongue should confess that Jesus Christ is Lord, to the glory of God the Father. (Philippians 2:10,11)**

We Must Know That:

The Beast is Recognized by 666

"Here is wisdom. Let him that hath understanding count the number of the beast: for it is the number of a man; and his number is Six hundred threescore and six." (Revelation 13:18)

THE IMAGE OF THE BEAST (6)

- **"And deceiveth them that dwell on the earth by the means of those miracles which he had power to do in the sight of the** *beast; saying to them that dwell on the earth, that they should make an image to the beast, which had the wound by a sword, and did live."* (Revelation 13:14)

- **The image of the beast is his personality to the world. The power he portrays to keep alive from his wound.**

THE MARK OF THE BEAST (6)

- The beast of the earth desires that all those who dwell on the earth, would wear the mark of the beast that rises up out of the sea.
- *"Saying to them that dwell on the earth".* (Revelation 13:14)
- ***The term (Them that dwell on the earth,) indicates those that are not in Christ.

This term does not refer to those that are saved in Christ. Because once we are in Christ, Paul tells us that the Father has placed us in heavenly places in Christ

Jesus. ***"Blessed be the God and Father of our Lord Jesus Christ, who hath blessed us with all spiritual blessings in heavenly places in Christ:"*** **(Ephesians 1:3)**

The beast of the earth succeeds with his desire by placing the mark of the beast on those who are not saved in Christ, or those who dwell in the earth. ***"And he causeth all, both small and great, rich and poor, free and bond, to receive a mark in their right hand, or in their foreheads"*** **(Revelation 13:16)**

Remember Christians wear the seal of the Holy Spirit until the day of redemption ***"And grieve not the Holy Spirit of God, whereby ye are sealed unto the day of redemption." **(Ephesians 4:30)**

THE NAME OF THE BEAST (6)

- **The name of the beast is highly praised by all those who do not know the Lord Jesus Christ. His name has power in the**

world, but not with Christians. This is his power to the world.

"And without controversy great is the mystery of godliness: God was manifest in the flesh, justified in the Spirit, seen of angels, preached unto the Gentiles, believed on in the world, received up into glory." (1 Timothy 3:16)